Parliamentary Representation

The Case of the
Norwegian
Storting

Donald R. Matthews and Henry Valen

Ohio State University Press
Columbus

Library of Congress Cataloging-in-Publication Data

Matthews, Donald R.
    Parliamentary representation : the case of the Norwegian Storting / Donald R.
Matthews and Henry Valen.
      p. cm.—(Parliaments and legislatures series)
    Includes bibliographical references (p.) and index.
    ISBN 0-8142-0798-7 (cloth : alk. paper). —ISBN 0-8142-5002-5
(pbk. : alk. paper)
    1. Norway. Stortinget. 2. Norway—Politics and government—1945–
3. Representative government and representation—Norway. I. Valen, Henry.
II. Title. III. Series.
JN7543.M38   1999
328.481'07347—dc21   98-35317
                                                     CIP

Cover design by Myungho Choi.
Type set in New Baskerville by Graphic Composition, Inc.
Printed by Thomson-Shore, Inc.

The paper used in this publication meets the minimum requirements of the
American National Standard for Information Sciences—Permanence of Paper for
Printed Library Materials. ANSI Z39.48–1992.

9   8   7   6   5   4   3   2   1

Parliaments and Legislatures Series

Samuel C. Patterson

General Advisory Editor

Contents

Foreword

The Norwegian Storting is a parliament of considerable fascination. It is a hoary parliamentary assembly, established after Norway separated from Denmark in 1814, whereupon a constitutional convention convened in Eidsvoll to forge a new basic law. Then and there, the fundamental design of Norway's national parliamentary institution was shaped. In 1884 electoral reforms transformed Norway into a modern parliamentary democracy. Interestingly, throughout this formative period Norway was in union with Sweden, and under the aegis of the Swedish king (until 1905).

The beige brick building in which parliament meets looks out on Løvebakken—Lion's Hill—in central Oslo. The main edifice is circular, mainly housing the parliamentary chambers where the Storting began meeting in 1866, braced by two rectangular extensions completed after World War II. The architecture of the parliament house is distinctively Scandinavian, and rather unlike any other legislative complex in the world.

Organizationally, the Norwegian parliament is a hybrid—not quite unicameral and not quite bicameral. As Donald Matthews and Henry Valen explain, all 165 members of the Storting are elected at the same time and in the same manner. But when the full postelection membership of the Storting assembles, the party caucuses determine how their members will be allocated between its two divisions, the Odelsting and the Lagting. Inside the parliament building are chambers for each of the two houses, separated by the Central Hall. In operation, the two houses operate in some ways in the manner of a bicameral parliament, with the smaller Lagting serving as a check on bills passed by the larger Odelsting.

Much of the time, Norway's parliament sustains a government—a prime minister and cabinet—with the direct support of only a minority of its members. The conventional wisdom, at least outside the Nordic countries, is that majority parties or coalitions in parliamentary systems elect and sustain governments. But Norway has enjoyed stable parliamentary democracy for many decades with minority governments (Norway is not alone in this; Sweden and Denmark commonly practice minority government too). The Christian Democratic government of Prime Minister Kjell Magne Bondevik, elected in September 1997, is based on the support of only 42 (the Christian Democratic members and their allies) of the 165 members of parliament. Although it is often assumed that minority governments are inherently unstable, the Norwegian case appears to contradict this assumption. On the contrary, since the Labor Party lost its Storting majority in 1961, in Norway minority and stable government is the rule, rather than the exception.

Commonly, when members of a parliament come to the chamber to take their seats they sit by political party. In European parliaments, this typically means that, as presiding officers look out on their chambers they see the leftist deputies (socialists, liberals) sitting to their left, and the right-wing representatives (conservatives, Christian democrats) sitting to their right. Here, the United States' practice is distinctively different from the European pattern: in the chambers of Congress, the Democrats, the party of the "left," sit to the right of the presiding officer, and the Republicans, the party of the "right," sit to the left of the dais. The Norwegian Storting presents a different mosaic as its members sit in the parliamentary chambers—they sit by county; the members for Møre og Romsdal sit together in a cluster of seats, the members for Sør-Trøndelag sit together in another cluster, the members for Rogaland sit in yet another cluster of seats, and so forth. At the same time, despite the constituency basis for seating in the parliamentary chamber, members vote almost exclusively on the basis of their political party affiliation.

Every complex political institution carries unusual or unique properties that make it especially fascinating to observe. Matthews and Valen dissect the Norwegian parliament with care, richly depicting its institutional peculiarities and powers. At the same time, the Storting is the institutional heart of a system of political representation in the European democratic mold. In their compelling account of political representation in Norway, Matthews and Valen demonstrate how empirically fruitful the case of Norway can be in illuminating the nexus between representatives and the represented. The authors ask, "How, and how well, does the Norwegian Storting represent the Norwegian people?" Their penetrating inquiry into Norway's institutional context, its elections and voting behavior, its political party performance and leadership, and its parliamentary membership and work provides a rich understanding of Norwegian politics. And the case of Norway contributes importantly to empirical theorizing about representative government more generally.

SAMUEL C. PATTERSON

Preface

This book grew out of our discovery during conversations in the early 1980s that we both were unhappy about the political science research on representation. Our discontents sprang from different backgrounds and career interests. Matthews, primarily a student of the United States and its Congress, felt that this research captured little of the realities of representation in the United States. Valen, an expert on Norwegian politics and elections, felt that existing models of political representation might be fine for the United States but were entirely inappropriate for Norway. After a time, we tired of criticizing the work of our friends and colleagues and decided to try to do better ourselves. This book is that attempt.

We chose to address the "paradox of representation" (Heinz Eulau's apt phrase) by conducting a study of how representation works in a single case, the Norwegian Storting, at one time in history, the late twentieth century. This permits us to study in considerable detail the way this one parliament represents, and fails to represent, the people. Our findings may or may not hold true for other legislatures at different times but our ultimate aim is to contribute to general, theoretical knowledge about political representation in many nations and times. This book is only a step in that direction.

We have written this book so that it could be of interest to disparate audiences—political scientists in Norway and elsewhere, but also journalists, politicians, and politically informed citizens. Thus we try to avoid technical language and use relatively simple statistics. In chapters 2 and 4 we present basic information about Norwegian politics and the Storting for beginners. Readers who are already familiar with these subjects can safely skip them.

Our study was based at the Institute for Social Research (ISR), Oslo. We are indebted to the institute for making their facilities available to us. The staff of the ISR program of electoral studies—Bernt Aardal, Gunnar

Vogt, Frode Berglund, and Hanne Marthe Narud—were very helpful to us in many ways. Narud was quite indispensable.

The Norwegian Social Science Data Services (NSD) provided additional data on political leaders, pubic opinion polls, and election surveys, as well as technical assistance and office space. Director Bjørn Henrichsen and his staff provided the highly professional service that social scientists have come to expect from NSD. Alte Alvheim was an outstanding adviser on analysis/computing problems at NSD.

Gudmund Hernes, a pioneer in parliamentary research in Norway (among many other things), encouraged us to engage in this project. He was especially helpful while we were formulating the questionnaire for the survey of Storting members.

Cheryl Mehaffey word-processed endless drafts of the manuscript cheerfully, rapidly and accurately, despite two authors who compose in barely legible longhand. Patrick Clarke converted our rough graphs into handsome line drawings.

Other persons who have helped along the way are Karen Anderson, the late John Ausland, Ann Buscherfeld, Ottar Hellevik, Stein Kuhnle, Donald McCrone, Lars Svåsand, and Paul Thyness.

The John Simon Guggenheim Memorial Foundation, the Norwegian Marshall Fund, and the University of Bergen–University of Washington Faculty Exchange Program provided financial support for Matthews's research trips to Norway. Valen is indebted to the Norwegian Research Council for Science and Humanities for granting him a senior fellowship that enabled him to pursue his work on this book. We wish to thank all these organizations for their very tangible expressions of confidence.

Finally, the following publishers were kind enough to grant us permission to quote from copyrighted material: Little, Brown and Company (an excerpt from Richard Fenno, *Home Style: House Members in Their District* [1978]); Sage Publications Ltd. (for reprinting much of Henry Valen's "Norway: Decentralization and Group Representation," in Michael Gallagher and Michael Marsh, eds., *Candidate Selection in Comparative Perspective: The Secret Garden of Politics* [1988]); Kluwer Academic Publishers (two figures from K. Strøm and J. Y. Leipart, "Ideology, Strategy and Party Competition," *European Journal of Political Research* 17 [1989]) and the University of Texas Press (for reprinting a table from R. E. Matland, "Institutional Variables Affecting Female Representation in National Legislators: The Case of Norway," *Journal of Politics* 55 [1993]).

Takk for hyggelig samarbeid.

Abbreviations

The following abbreviations have been used in the text, tables, and figures.

ALP	Anders Langes Party
BP	Agrarian Party or Farmers Party
DNA	Labor Party
EC or EU	European Community
FrP	Progress Party
H	Conservative Party
KrF	Christian People's Party
LO	Norwegian Federation of Trade Unions
NATO	North Atlantic Treaty Organization
NKP	Communist Party
PR	Proportional Representation
SD	Social Democratic Party
SF	Socialist Electoral Alliance
SP	Center Party
SV	Socialist Left Party
V	Liberal Party

1

Introduction

This is a book about the Norwegian Parliament and how it represents the Norwegian people.

The reasons for our interest in this subject may not be self-evident. Norway is a small country on the periphery of Europe, and its 4.5 million people are of little significance on the world's geo-political stage. The Storting[1] is an ordinary sort of legislature, similar to the national legislatures of many other small democracies and to many subnational assemblies. Like all legislatures in modern times, the Storting is sometimes criticized as increasingly irrelevant and powerless in grappling with the problems of the late twentieth century. Why, then, study the Storting?

Studying how the Storting represents the Norwegian people is a good way to learn more about how representative government works in general. The smallness of Norway, the ordinariness of the Storting have advantages for exploring this question. The complexities of larger systems—racial, ethnic, and religious conflicts, in addition to economic ones, and complex, multilayered governments—are avoided. It is easier to see how representative government works in smaller countries. And this is a first step toward understanding representative government in general, a big and important question that is not well understood.

Without representation popular government would be impossible today. The direct self-government of the Greek city-states or the New England towns was abandoned long ago in favor of indirect government by surrogates. While a few elements of direct democracy persist (see Cronin, 1989; Butler and Ranney, 1994), and while modern electronic technology makes it physically possible to involve millions of people in politics through mass communications and opinion surveys (Arterton, 1987), the size of today's political units combined with the number and complexity of governmental problems makes direct democracy inconceivable or unwise. A few men and women rule, everyone else is ruled. The relationships between the two are what concern us.

Virtually all contemporary governments claim to be representative. Governments cannot long rule by coercion alone, thus governors *say* they represent the masses and provide at least some of what they think the populace wants—be it prosperity, justice, military triumphs, scapegoats, whatever—in order to encourage mass acquiescence and their own survival. But true representative government is more than this.

The Concept of Political Representation

Definitions of political representation abound (e.g., Pitkin, 1967; Pennock and Chapman, 1968; Eulau and Wahlke, 1978). Pitkin, after an exhaustive analysis of the multiple uses of the term, writes: "Political representation is primarily a public, institutionalized arrangement involving many people and groups and operating in the complex ways of large scale social arrangements. What makes it representation is not any single action by any one participant, but the overall structure and functioning of the system, the patterns emerging from the multiple activities of many people. It is representation if the people (or a constituency) are present in governmental action, even though they do not literally act for themselves" (221–22). Somewhat more concretely she concludes that representation "means acting in the interest of the represented, in a manner responsive to them" (209).

Representative governments are characterized by institutions and practices that increase the chances of achieving this condition—invariably including free, popular, and competitive elections, but also many other arrangements. These institutions and practices vary widely; their fine details make a difference. This book focuses upon how such institutions and practices affect the process of representation in Norway.

Historically, legislative bodies have played a central role in the achievement of representative democracy. They have been viewed as the premier representative institution ever since. Most studies of representation, including this one, focus on how legislatures or legislators represent the absent others. In this era of executive-centered government, however, this leaves out many powerful political actors—cabinet ministers, bureaucrats, judges, commissioners, consultants, and the like—who are engaged in political representation, too. Unfortunately, we cannot study them all in this work. How and how well the Norwegian Parliament represents the Norwegian people is, by itself, a surprisingly complex question.

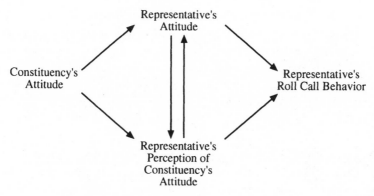

Figure 1.1 The Miller-Stokes Model of Representative Process. *Source:* Miller and Stokes (1963), 50, fig. 1.

Previous Research on Representation

Most empirical research on representation has been conducted by American political scientists on American legislatures, assuming Anglo-American conditions—two-party systems, single-member electoral districts, first-past-the-post elections, and so on.[2] Most democratic national legislatures, including the Norwegian Storting, are differently organized. The result is that the models and methods used to study representation in the United States are not always helpful in comprehending representation in other legislatures.

Warren Miller and Donald Stokes's 1963 article "Constituency Influence in Congress" has had a profound effect on subsequent empirical research on political representation. They explain the representative process using the model presented in figure 1.1. Members of Congress, in the model, vote for or against legislative proposals on the basis of their own policy preferences or their perception of their constituents' preferences. These two variables can interact—the members' personal policy attitudes can color how they see the views of others, the perceived policy preferences of constituents can be so strong and clear that legislators may (perhaps unwittingly, perhaps intentionally) adopt them as their own. But no matter what, both the legislators' personal preferences and their perceptions of the preferences of their constituents are profoundly affected by the preferences of constituents. Members of congress are popularly elected and presumably hold popular policy views; the members' perceptions of popular opinion and actual popular opinion may not be identical, but regular misinterpretation of constituency opinion is likely to lead to electoral defeat.

This article was a giant advance in the empirical study of representation. But, like all models, it is a simplified version of reality. And it is far less useful in understanding legislative representation outside the United States than in the American Congress. Note some of its limitations:

- The analysis concerns individual members of Congress and their relationship with their constituents in geographically defined single-member districts. This fits the American context, but in systems with different institutional arrangements—multimember districts and proportional representation, for example—it is not appropriate.

- Representation becomes congruence between the issue preferences of constituents (all of them? a majority of them?) and the votes of their representatives. This assumes that constituents have preferences on public policy, that these preferences can be made known to legislators in a timely fashion, and that those mass preferences can be compared to the highly specific and sometimes technical decisions that legislating requires. It assumes that the legislators' votes on issues are the only thing that matters in judging how representative a legislature is. (For contrary views, see Cnudde and McCrone, 1966; Wahlke, 1971; Matthews and Stimson, 1975; Weissberg, 1978, 1979.) Nor does it link the preferences of voters to public policy outcomes of legislative actions.

- Finally, the direction of causality is assumed to be from the constituency to the legislators' vote. Given the differences in political attention, interest, and sophistication between full-time politicians and other people, this assumption is not an easy one to accept (Wahlke, 1971).

Other empirical research on representation provides some correctives. Wahlke et al.'s *The Legislative System* (1962), a comparative study of four American state legislatures, views legislatures as systems of roles, or norms of behavior. The two most important of their role orientations for our purposes are representational-role orientation and area-role orientation. Wahlke and his collaborators classify the representational role orientations of members as "trustees" (who, following Edmund Burke, claim to vote their personal convictions and principles), "delegates" (who stress their responsibility to respond to their constituents), and "politicos" (who pursue a mixed strategy). Members also differ in how they define their constituency: some think they ought to represent the entire state, others just their electoral districts, and still others some mixture of the two. The important point of this work, which has been widely replicated in all manner of legislatures, using all manner of measurement instruments (see Jewell, 1970), is this: legislators define for themselves, at least to some degree, whom they represent and how.

Richard Fenno's *Home Style: House Members in Their Districts* (1978), based upon seven years of observation of eighteen members of the U.S. House of Representatives, adds much substance to that perspective. When members look at their districts, Fenno suggests, they see their constituencies as "a nest of concentric circles" (1), the largest of which is the legally defined geographical district. Within this, the members see the people in the district who they think voted for them—their re-election constituency. Within this are their strongest supporters—the primary constituency—and a small circle of intimates, the personal constituency. Fenno's description and analysis of the relationships between members of Congress and these different constituencies is too detailed and complex to summarize here, but it suggests a great deal about the process of representation. We quote at length:

> This is the view from over the congressman's shoulder: nearly everything he does to win and hold support—allocating, reaching, presenting, responding, communicating, explaining, assuring—involves representation. It is a view of representation as a process. It is a view of representation as politics, with all of the uncertainties of politics. It is a view, however, that has the net effect of making representation less policy-centered than it usually is. Traditionally, representation has been treated mostly as a structural relationship in which the congruence between the policy preferences of the represented and the policy decisions of the representative is the measure of good representation. . . . But we need to know, as well, the answer to an intertwining question: "How does Representative X win and hold his or her district?" And to answer it we shall need to consider more than policy preferences and policy agreements. . . .
>
> We shall have to consider the possibility that supportive constituents may want extra policy behavior from their representatives. They may want good access or the assurance of good access as much as they want good policy. They may want "a good man" or "a good woman," someone whose assurances they can trust, as much as they want good policy. They

may want communication promises as much as they want policy promises. The point is not that policy preferences are not a crucial basis for
the representational relationship. They are. The point is that we should
not start our studies of representation by assuming they are the only
basis for a representational relationship. They are not. (240–41)

David Mayhew's *Congress: The Electoral Connection* (1974) is another
work that has had much influence on how American scholars look at representation. What if, Mayhew asks, members of Congress were first and
foremost concerned with achieving their own re-election? How would
they behave? How would Congress as an institution look? Mayhew makes
a convincing case that the Congress and members of Congress would look
about the way it does now. Members keep their constituents content by
aggressively championing constituents' interests in their parochial dealings with the executive (see also Fiorina, 1977), by "position-taking" (saying things that constituents want to hear without doing anything about
them), and by "credit-claiming" (claiming to have contributed to desirable collective outcomes). Responding to specific expressed policy
preferences of constituents does not loom very large in the relationship
between members of Congress and their constituents as depicted in this
seminal work. Much of what members of Congress do is purely symbolic,
having little to do with policy or legislation.

Another theme in the recent literature suggests that all these studies
are too individualistic. What really matters is whether or how legislators
collectively represent the people *collectively* (Eulau and Prewitt, 1973; Eulau
and Karps, 1977; Weissberg, 1978, 1979). Do subgroups within parliaments represent groups of constituents? These seem to be central questions that have received little attention (but see Eulau and Prewitt, 1973;
Holmberg, 1974; Loewenberg and Kim, 1978; Esaiasson and Holmberg,
1996).

Finally, empirical research on political representation tends to be
static and ahistorical. It usually examines the policy preferences of voters
and the real or alleged response (or nonresponse) of elected officials at
a single point in time. The technology of research encourages this perspective—sample surveys provide snapshots of mass opinion, not moving
pictures. And yet, a view that representation is a dynamic process characterized by leadership, delayed response, and change over long time periods is very persuasive (Stimson, 1991).

All of this suggests the desirability of new and perhaps more complex
models than Miller-Stokes to study political representation. We still need

models, but ones that are more helpful to understanding the complexities of real-world representation, especially outside the United States.

Approach of This Study

How, then, do we approach the study of political representation in Norway?

The Concept of Responsiveness: A Second Look

Like most other scholars in this field, we accept the responsiveness definition of representation. But responsiveness is not an easy thing to prove. The "law of anticipatory reaction" (Friedrick, 1941) is a confounding factor: legislators can and do anticipate the probable policy preferences of constituents even when constituents do not have any or fail to communicate those they do have. Moreover, legislators can and do create and shape mass policy preferences as well as react to them.

Thus, agreement between representatives and constituents by itself does not demonstrate responsiveness. Rather, there are several possible explanations of such agreement:

> the followers influenced the leader;
> the leader influenced the followers;
> the leader and followers both influenced each other;
> both leader and followers were influenced by a third factor—
>   a shared ideology, for example;
> the process of selecting leaders results in leader-follower
>   agreement thereafter, without further communication.

Agreement by itself does not tell which of these explanations apply. Thus we shall look beyond the degree of agreement between representatives and the represented to the processes of representation and how those processes may encourage or inhibit agreement.

Types of Representation

Legislative representation can be studied at several levels. We can examine how well the legislature as a whole represents the people as a whole

Type of Responsiveness

Level of Representation	Policy	Service	Symbolic
Aggregate	Lawmaking Budgeting Oversight	Allocation of particularized benefits through collective action	Symbolic legislation Symbolic representation of voters by members
Individual	Committee work Debating on floor	Services provided to constituents by individual members	Position-taking Credit-claiming

Figure 1.2 Types of Legislative Representation

(aggregate representation) or how well the individual legislator represents his or her constituency (dyadic representation). And legislators (either individually or collectively) can respond to their constituents in a variety of ways. They can work to further the policy preferences of their constituents by introducing legislation, persuading colleagues in debate, casting votes, and so on. These activities are certainly at the core of the process of representation, and it is this *policy representation* that will primarily concern us in this book. But legislators respond in additional ways to needs and desires of the absent others. Members of legislatures can and do devote considerable time and energy to securing particularized benefits for individuals and groups within their constituencies. They work, and work hard, to bring more general benefit to their constituencies as a whole. These activities may have little or nothing to do with legislation or public policy, but they are a significant part of representative government. We call this *service representation*. Finally, legislators (either individually or collectively) engage in behavior that generates trust and support among the represented. Representative government cannot survive without diffuse support from the citizenry. Individual legislators often feel that voter trust is a necessary if not sufficient condition to re-election. Symbolic behavior that generates such feelings and attitudes is a third part of the representative relationship. We call those activities *symbolic representation*.

Combining the two levels of representation with these types of responsiveness, one ends up with the six types of legislative representation presented in figure 1.2. While dealing with six types of representation is a lot more complicated than considering only one, it should result in a more realistic description and analysis than simpler approaches. And, fortunately for the analyst, real-life political systems tend to stress some forms of representation more than others. Aggregate representation is emphasized in the Norwegian Storting and other legislatures like it, while political individualism holds sway in the United States, and most Anglo-American legislatures. Thus this book is primarily concerned with aggregate-level representation.

The Process of Representation

Political representation is a process. What does that process look like? How do political institutions and practices shape the process? How well does the process lead to the representation of the absent others in parliamentary decisions? Those are the questions we seek to answer about the Norwegian Parliament. Three models of the representative process offer contrasting answers. Each is a different way of looking at legislative representation.

THE PARTY MANDATE MODEL. Probably the most popular image of how legislative representation works is the party government or party mandate model. According to this model, political parties develop public policies and nominate candidates, the voters choose between the parties, and the victorious party or parties carries out the mandates upon election to the legislature. Thus, the interests and opinions of the people are represented (APSA, 1950; Ranney, 1962).

Norwegian realities complicate this model. The country has had more than two political parties throughout the twentieth century—usually five or six major ones. The last time a single political party won a majority in the Storting was 1957. Coalition governments and minority governments are the norm. Thus, while the multiplicity of political parties provides the voter with an array of choices, individual political parties are seldom able to implement their policy pledges in the Storting without gaining the support of Storting members of competing political parties elected with different policy mandates. The compromises and bargains struck in this process of government formation and lawmaking thus weakens the linkage between the policy preferences of party voters and the public policies that ultimately emerge.

Norway also employs calendar elections: Storting elections occur every four years. Old issues fade, new issues surge to prominence between elections. Governments and parliaments must react to changed circum-

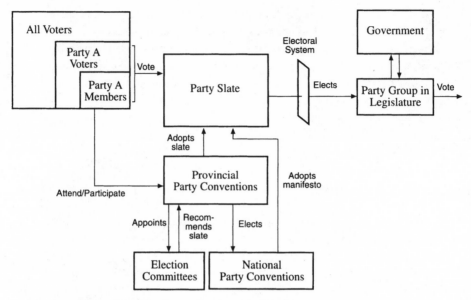

Figure 1.3   The Party Mandate Model of Representative Process

stances—a worldwide depression, the collapse of a superpower, domestic crises, etc.—that electoral mandates cannot anticipate. In the fast-changing world of the late twentieth century, this further delimits the utility of periodic electoral mandates as indicators of contemporary mass preferences.

The process by which voter preferences are converted into public policy through party mandates is schematically depicted in figure 1.3. For a single, hypothetical Norwegian party, the diagram shows how the preferences of party voters are transformed into public policy via party mandates; of course, the same transformation takes place within all the other parties as well, until all voters are represented in the Storting.

For the party mandate model to work so that public policies reflect the opinions of the electorate quite a number of conditions must hold. To list a few: party voters must vote for their party slate because of their agreement with the party's manifesto or platform on public issues; parties must provide voters an opportunity to vote for or against different policies by developing clear and competing manifestos; and Storting members must be bound by their respective party manifestos. Whether these conditions prevail is of critical importance to the party mandate theory. In chapters 6 and 7, we shall examine how well these conditions and assumptions hold true in contemporary Norway.

THE CORPORATE PLURALISM MODEL. Norwegian politics is usually described as corporatist—private groups are more thoroughly incorporated, formally and informally, into the governmental process than in most other countries (Rokkan, 1966; Kvavik, 1976). When this mode of interest group mediation is applied to the Storting, it results in a corporatist style of legislative representation. Nonparty interest groups are its significant actors, and they seek political power through inclusion within the legislature. The result is political representation.

The democratization of politics in Norway was both cause and effect of the opening of the Storting to members of new, previously powerless groups—farmers, industrial workers, women, and young people. The more the Storting approaches being an average assortment of ordinary Norwegians, according to this model, the more political representation there will be. Nominating processes—how group members get on party lists—is especially important for this type of representation. This will be examined in chapter 5. In chapter 8 we examine the social and economic characteristics of Storting members and the consequences of their backgrounds for symbolic and policy representation.

But not all interest groups can be represented in the Storting by members or even fellow travelers. In a free society, this results in a more competitive and pluralistic style of interest group politics existing alongside the corporatist one. Groups outside the formal boundaries of the legislature are represented as well. How this works in Norway is explored in chapter 9.

The combination of both corporatist and pluralist processes in a single state we call corporate pluralism, a concept introduced by Stein Rokkan (1966).

THE PRINCIPAL-AGENT MODEL. The third model of the representative process that we shall employ in this book—the principal-agent model—has recently migrated into political science from microeconomic and organization theory (see Barro, 1973; Ferejohn, 1986; Kiewiet and McCubbins, 1991; Krehbiel, 1992; Parker, 1992; Arnold, 1993). It likens political representation to the delegation of authority from a principal (a business manager, for example) to an agent (say, a worker in the manager's firm). The model assumes that both principals and agents behave as rational, goal-seeking egoists. This results in inevitable conflicts of interest between principals and agents. How then can principals control the behavior of agents despite the superior information of the agents (they do the job every day) and limited attention and supervision from principals (who delegate their authority in one area so as to devote their time and attention to something else)? Principal-agent theorists suggest a variety of approaches that can be used by principals to maintain control. Contracts that motivate agents to serve the principals' interests, careful screening and selection of agents, monitoring and reporting requirements, and institutional checks and balances all can make it possible for an intermittently attentive principal to control, within limits, the behavior of agents. The resulting division of labor and specialization leads to great efficiencies. Kiewiet and McCubbins conclude:

> We thus find it inconceivable that . . . large organizations could achieve their collective aims without engaging in prodigious amounts of delegation.
>
> Certainly, the benefits derived from delegation come at a price. The principal suffers welfare losses caused by opportunistic behavior on the part of his or her agents. . . . There is available to this principal, however, a large repertoire of mechanisms for reducing agency losses. . . . The degree to which the principal's strategies are effective should therefore never be inferred from the amount of time, energy, and attention the principal devotes to them. (37–38)

This perspective can be applied to the Norwegian political scene. The ultimate principals are, of course, the voters. When they vote for one of Norway's political parties they delegate their political authority to that party for the next four years. These voters need not follow political events closely but must be able to judge the desirability of outcomes of partisan politics. Every four years they must decide whether to continue delegating authority to the same party or switch to a different one. Voting is thus mostly retrospective, based upon past performance, and does not require a sophisticated understanding of policy issues. Even so, according to principal-agent theory, it is possible for the voters to control what governments do (within acceptable levels of slippage below complete control) if this delegation is properly done. Among the necessary, if not sufficient, conditions for successful delegation in this context would seem to be free, fair, and regular elections; several political parties that aggressively campaign for support; and political parties that seek to preserve and expand their electoral followings.

The delegation of political authority from voters to parties is only the first level of delegation in a popular system. The Norwegian political parties delegate their authority to their candidates, or more precisely to those candidates they nominate who are elected to the Storting. The effective principals in this delegation are the local and provincial party activists who control party nominations. They are far more politically attentive and knowledgeable than the average voter. But, then, elected members of the Storting are prominent and popular people, they deal with complex issues, and much of what they do is done in the privacy of committee and caucus rooms. Thus control over Storting members is neither easy nor automatic.

Nonetheless, it is critically important to the party that its agents in the Storting perform as a team and avoid potentially unpopular actions. Certain types of candidates are probably easier for the parties to control—persons who have proven to be faithful and responsible party members in the past, who want to serve in the Storting for extended periods, who do not have great personal popularity independent of their party position, and so on. The process of nomination can also facilitate control if it is highly competitive and the threat of involuntary removal (or demotion on the electoral list) is plausible, even if infrequently exercised.

In a popular system of government, principal-agent delegation goes on considerably beyond this point. The most important of these delegations is the choice of the government by the Storting. This, of course, involves a tremendous delegation of authority by the parliamentary party or parties represented in the government. This delegation does not represent total abdication; Norwegian governments are entirely dependent on the Storting for new legislation and budgetary support. A government that cannot win consistent majority support in the Storting is finished. Negotiations between the government and other agents of the parliamentary parties—party leaders, members of the Storting's Council of Presidents, and the standing committees—are nearly continuous.

Thus, the process of legislative representation in Norway can be thought of as a nested set of principal-agent relationships. All the principals, by definition, possess the authority to remove agents if they do not serve the principals' objectives. The agents, however, have their own goals and seek to retain independence to pursue them successfully (Parker, 1992). But there are many strategies and devices that principals can use to maintain an acceptable level of control. In chapters 5, 6, 7, and 9, we shall examine the utility of this model.

One final word on these process models. Our purpose is not to prove or disprove the truth or falsehood of these models but to use them as ways to comprehend representation. A model may not be an accurate depiction of Norwegian realities but still can raise interesting questions about why representation in Norway diverges from it.

The Data

The analysis in this book has been based upon four sets of data:

1. A representative voter survey conducted immediately after the Storting election of September 1985. The study, which was undertaken at the Institute for Social Research in Oslo and directed by Henry Valen and Bernt Aardal, is based upon a nationwide probability sample of 2,967 voters. Interviews were obtained with 2,180, a response rate of 74 percent. The fieldwork was conducted by the survey division of the Central Bureau of Statistics in Oslo.[3]

2. A mail survey of members of nomination committees in all constituencies. These committees, which hold a key position in the process of nomination, are appointed by the province board of the respective parties. National party leaders and bureaucracy do not know who the members of the nomination committees are. Consequently, our questionnaire had to be administered through the secretariats of the provincial party organizations. The fieldwork, which was organized by the Institute for Social Research, was conducted in the summer of 1985, before the Storting election. Of a total 920 committee members, 548 returned the questionnaire, a response rate of about 60 percent.

3. A mail survey to the members of the Storting, 1985–89. The questionnaire was sent to the representatives in the spring of 1988. Of the 157 representatives, 147, or 94 percent, responded. The study was organized by the Institute for Social Research.

4. Biographical data of Storting representatives, 1945–85. Information on the backgrounds of representatives has been collected by the Storting and was made available in machine-readable form through the Norwegian Social Science Data Service.

Copies of the questionnaires are available in Norwegian or English translation from the Norwegian Social Science Data Service, Bergen, N-5014 Norway.

The major data sets used in this study are now a decade old. Since our interest is in describing how political representation works, rather than describing contemporary events, we do not believe that this seriously affects our findings. When possible we have updated time series into the 1990s from other sources.

What began as a seemingly simple question—how does the Norwegian Parliament represent the Norwegian people?—turns out to be very complex. In order to deal with this question, we argue that one must distinguish between policy, service, and symbolic representation, and between individual and aggregate levels of representation. We also have suggested three different models of the ways in which legislatures come to reflect the desires of citizens—the party mandate, corporate-pluralist, and principal-agent models. We look at several different types of representation through several theoretical-conceptual lenses. The result is a richness and depth of view that we could not otherwise achieve.

2

Norwegian Politics: An Introduction

R epresentative government in Norway began with the Constitution of
1814. When the four-hundred-year union with Denmark was dissolved in the aftermath of the Napoleonic Wars, the Norwegians seized
the opportunity to declare national independence and to write their own
constitution. Although the country subsequently was forced to accept a
union with Sweden, it retained its Constitution and its domestic independence even while under the Swedish king.

The constitutional assembly of 1814 was faced with an extraordinary
challenge. The absolutist Danish-Norwegian monarchy had to be replaced by a new regime. Models to emulate were few. The assembly was
acquainted with and influenced by the liberal ideas expressed in the
French Revolutionary Constitution of 1793 and the American Constitution of 1789. Another source of inspiration was the Swedish Government
Reform of 1809. Since the task was to restore Norway as an independent
state, the assembly looked for national traditions that predated the union
with Denmark. Thus, traces of thirteenth-century law and custom may be
seen in the 1814 Constitution as well.[1]

The resulting document was one of the most liberal constitutions of its
time. "The Constitution is a remarkable document," wrote Stein Rokkan,
"remarkable for what it tells us about the ideals and the strategies of the
elite at the time, but equally remarkable for the possibilities it opened up
for future developments" (1966: 369). The Constitution did not include
a specific declaration of rights, but the principles of civil rights, due process of law, and freedom of speech were honored in a number of para-
graphs. The principle of separation of powers also was laid down in the
Constitution: monarchy was maintained, but royal power was restricted
by the power of the two other branches of government, the legislative and
the judicial. Most important from the point of view of political representation were the liberal suffrage rules. About 45 percent of the adult male

population, including freeholding farmers, were given the right to vote in the indirect election of Storting members.

The Constitution of 1814 is still in effect, although with a number of amendments, some written and some accepted through constitutional practice (*sedvane*). The political system has changed greatly over the years, and so have the forms and conditions for political representation. Two major reforms were crucial: the introduction of parliamentary government and the emergence of a party system.

Origins of Parliamentary Government

The system created in 1814 allowed for continued rule by the class of civil servants inherited from the Danish-Norwegian monarchy. In addition to staffing the public bureaucracy, civil servants were elected to the Storting in great numbers. This upper class of public officials and urban patricians constituted less than 2 percent of the electorate. However, the Constitution set the stage for opposition and protest from the still inarticulate strata of the population.

The first signs of opposition occurred around 1830, inspired by the July Revolution in France. Although political campaigning was seen as immoral in those days, a group of urban liberals launched a campaign at the 1832 Storting election, resulting in the election of a majority of farmers to the Storting. But this had only limited and temporary political effects. The next wave of opposition, triggered by the revolutionary events of 1848 in Europe, was of more lasting significance. A socialist organization for workers and tenant farmers was established, Thranitterbevegelsen, named after its leader, Marcus Thrane. Although its most important demand was universal suffrage, the organization was accused of revolutionary activities. Its leaders were convicted and sentenced to long jail sentences.

These new ideas, however, also affected people who were already enfranchised. An alliance emerged in the Storting between the farmers and a group of urban radicals led by lawyers (*sakforere*) and therefore called Sakforerpartiet. The farmers gave electoral strength to this opposition, but the urban radicals provided the ideas, mainly demands for democratic reforms. In 1859, an attempt was made to form a political party in the Storting, Reformforeningen (Reform Association). But organized political activities were still frowned upon, and the attempt had to be abandoned. Around 1870, the two opposition groups once more joined forces in a demand for constitutional change. They proposed that it should be mandatory for members of the government to meet with the Storting to defend their policies. Consistent with the constitutional principle of separation of powers, the king and the government refused to accept this proposal. A long struggle, lasting through the 1870s, ensued. The Storting became highly polarized. The opposition forces were called Venstre (the Left), while those who supported the establishment were called Høyre (the Right). A party system existed in all but name.

The Storting election of 1882, which was the first clear-cut partisan election in Norway, resulted in an overwhelming majority for the Left. This majority was able to have the Storting impeach the government for not complying with the decisions of the Storting.[2] In the impeachment of 1884 the government was forced to leave office, and the king was compelled to ask the leader of the Left to form a new government. This was the beginning of parliamentary government in Norway. Curiously, the principle of parliamentarism has never been written into the Constitution. It has been established only through constitutional practice.

Development of the Party System

Parliamentary government implies party government. It is hardly conceivable that a parliamentary regime could be maintained without organized political parties of some kind. Parties are required for mobilizing competing political elites and for organizing their electoral support. Thus, it was no coincidence that the two first parties in Norway, Venstre and Høyre, were formally organized in 1884 immediately after the introduction of parliamentarism.

From the start the Left Party was socially and ideologically diverse. After an overwhelming electoral victory in 1885, the party was torn apart by conflict over religious questions. In 1888, a fundamentalist wing broke off and formed the Moderate Left Party. In coalition with the Right, this party opposed the Pure Left for more than a decade.

Economic modernization started relatively late in Norway; the country remained a rural society until the turn of the century. Then all of a sudden the development of hydroelectric power—Norway has many rivers and waterfalls—triggered a process of rapid industrialization. This process radically altered the political landscape as well as the economy. The Labor Party, which had been formed in 1887, remained a small political sect until 1903, when it won its first Storting seats. From then on, its support increased sharply from one election to the next.

An industrial proletariat—fully enfranchised in 1898—became a major target in the competition between the political parties. Venstre radicalized its platform, advocating new social reforms benefiting the new lower classes as well as strict policies protecting natural resources from exploitation by foreign and Norwegian capitalists. Further, in the years after 1906, Venstre carried out a consolidation by forcing moderate elements to leave the party. Those who left Venstre either joined a new party, Frisinnede Venstre (the Liberal Left), or moved over to Høyre. The latter party changed from being largely a party of civil servants to include also a strong contingent of businessmen.

The first two decades of the twentieth century were also a period of increasing class differences. In the Labor Party, which originally had been rather moderate, a radical wing emerged in 1911 (Fagopposisjonen). At the time of the Russian Revolution this wing turned revolutionary and became a majority in the party. When the Labor Party in 1919 joined the Communist International, or Comintern, the moderate wing broke off and formed a Social Democratic Party. But the Norwegian Labor Party soon began to disagree with the International. In 1923, the Comintern demanded that all national member parties should be reorganized in accordance with Marxist-Leninist principles and subordinate to decisions of the International. Labor had had enough and left the Comintern. But a small wing broke off to form a separate Communist Party. For a few years the country had three competing socialist parties, but in 1927 Labor and the Social Democrats managed to reunite and won a convincing victory in the subsequent election (38 percent of the votes).

The period around 1920 also was characterized by great political unrest and volatility in the bourgeois camp.[3] The agricultural sector had changed from largely subsistence farming to a market economy. In 1920 a new Agrarian Party was formed, which drew most of its support from farmers who previously had voted for one of two other bourgeois parties. Since the Labor Party had become the dominant force of the left, Venstre had to accept its new role as a party of the center.

Eventually Norway had a system of five parties. From left to right the parties were: the Communists, Labor, the Liberal Party (Venstre), the Agrarian Party, and the Conservative Party (Høyre). However, as early as 1933 a new party emerged among religious fundamentalists on the west coast, the Christian People's Party, which became a sixth nationwide party after World War II.

The period after World War II was characterized by great political stability. The Labor Party held governmental power from 1945 to 1965, despite losing its majority in the Storting in 1961. In that year, a neutralist party was formed in opposition to the Cold War, the Socialist People's Party, ideologically located between Labor and the Communists. In the Storting election of 1961 the party obtained two seats, enough to deny Labor a majority.

During most of the postwar period, the four bourgeois parties were scattered along several dimensions of conflict. The Labor Party leaders claimed that there was no government alternative to Labor. But in the summer of 1963 a cabinet crisis occurred due to an accident in the state-owned coal mines on Spitsbergen. The bourgeois parties managed to form a coalition, which lasted just 28 days. Nonetheless, the bourgeois parties had demonstrated that they could form a government, and in the election of 1965 they obtained a joint majority in the Storting and subsequently formed a coalition government with the Agrarian leader, Per Borten, as prime minister. From then on, two government alternatives existed: either a minority Labor government or a bourgeois coalition.

The 1970s were a divisive period in Norwegian politics due to the debate over Norway's entry into the European Community (EC). Despite support from the country's two largest political parties, membership was rejected in a referendum held in September 1972. After the referendum, major changes occurred in the party system. The old, distinguished Venstre split into two mini-parties and temporarily disappeared.[4] On the left wing, the Communist Party, the Socialist People's Party, and an anti-EC wing of the Labor Party formed a Socialist Electoral Alliance, which later (1975) became the Socialist Left Party. However, the most remarkable event was the establishment in 1973 of a right-wing populist party, called Anders Langes Party after the name of the founder.[5] This event was not directly related to the EC issue, but the party profited greatly from the hostilities created during the acrimonious debate on Europe. In 1976, after the death of the founder, the party took the name Progress Party.

Dimensions of Political Conflict

In order to understand the party system, it is useful to look at the underlying structural cleavages around which the parties developed. We may distinguish between six cleavages (Rokkan and Valen, 1964; Rokkan, 1967; Valen and Rokkan, 1974):

1. A territorial cleavage between the central region and two distinct peripheries, the North and the Southwest;
2. Three cultural cleavages, articulated by three countercultures—the language movement, the temperance movement, and the lay religious movement—and their corresponding urban cultures:
   a. the sociocultural conflict over language;
   b. a moral cleavage concerning moral legislation, particularly regarding sale and production of alcoholic beverages;
   c. a religious cleavage concerning the control of the Lutheran State Church;
3. Two economic cleavages:
   a. the conflict in the labor market between workers and employers;
   b. the conflict in the commodity market between producers and consumers of products from the primary sector of the economy.

In table 2.1, the development of the party system since 1882 is broken down into eight different periods. For each of these stages we report the most important events that shaped politics, the major parties contesting elections, and which of the six political cleavages were salient. For example, the first phase, which occurred between 1882 and 1885, was dominated by the struggle for party government, the major parties were the Left and the Right, and territorial and sociocultural cleavages were dominant. Looking down the table, we see the events, parties, and cleavages change until we arrive at the eighth and most contemporary phase with its six parties (seven including the Liberals) and all six cleavages manifested in contemporary politics.

"The severity of these cleavages," Kaare Strøm wrote, "should not be over-estimated. In a sense, these political conflicts dominate the scene by default, since there exist no truly fundamental divisions" (1990: 202). There are no racial minorities (save for a very small number of Lapps, or Sámis). Norway is overwhelmingly Protestant, income inequality is modest, the sense of national identity strong. Outside observers are more impressed by Norway's homogeneity than by its divisions, although it has and needs both (Eckstein, 1966).

Party Structure

In his classic work on political parties, Maurice Duverger (1954) proposed the hypothesis that party structure is determined by the prevailing

Table 2.1
Stages of Party Development

Phase	Conditioning Events	Elections	Major Party Alternatives									Cleavages*					
												T	SC	M	R	LM	CM
I	Struggle for parliamentary government	1882–85					V			H		X	X	X	X		
II	Victory of the Left, extension of suffrage	1888–97					V			H		X	X	X	X		
III	Manhood suffrage, struggle over union with Sweden	1900–15			DNA		V			H		X	X	X	X	X	
IV	Industrialization, proportional representation	1918–30	NKP		DNA	SD	V		BP	H		X	X	X	X	X	
V	Great Depression	1933–36	NKP		DNA		V	KrF	BP	H		X	X	X	X	X	
VI	Recovery from World War II	1945–57	NKP		DNA		V	KrF	BP	H		X	X	X	X	X	
VII	Cold War, international policies	1961–69	NKP	SF	DNA		V	KrF	SP**	H		X	X	X	X	X	
VIII	Struggle over EC membership	1973–	SV		DNA		V	KrF	SP	H	ALP/FrP***	X	X	X	X	X	X

*T = territorial cleavage, SC = sociocultural cleavage, M = moral cleavage, R = religious cleavage, LM = labor market cleavage, CM = commodity market cleavage.

**In 1959 the Farmers Party (BP) changed its name to Center Party (SP).

***Anders Langes Party, founded in 1973, changed its name to Progress Party in 1977.

circumstances and demands at the time when the party was founded. Parties maintain their original structure, and, consequently, highly different types of parties can exist side by side in the same society. Most relevant for our purpose is his distinction between caucus parties and mass parties. Caucus parties are the old bourgeois parties, which were founded in the latter half of the nineteenth century. Their organization is weak and inactive between elections, according to Duverger. The center of power in these parties is located in the parliamentary caucus. Mass parties, on the other hand, are characterized by strong and active organizations. Socialist parties formed in the twentieth century fit this type best. In these parties, parliamentary activities are largely subordinate to decisions made by the membership organizations.

Later students of political parties have tended to disagree with Duverger (McKenzie, 1955; Ranney and Kendall, 1956; Epstein, 1967). Their thesis is that parties acquire an organizational structure fitting the political institutions within which they function. Thus, despite differences in policies and ideological outlook, parties of a given country tend to be similar in organizational structure.

This second view fits the Norwegian case well. Although the Norwegian parties emerged gradually over a period of nearly one hundred years, their structure today is similar, at least on a formal level. The two oldest parties emerged within the Storting around 1880; their mass organizations were established in 1884 after the introduction of parliamentary government. Consistent with the Duverger hypothesis, their organizations seem to have been rather weak. This may, for example, be observed in the area of local politics. In order to maintain viable organizations on the grass-roots level, a party needs to run lists at local elections. But except for urban communes, the bourgeois parties failed to run straight partisan lists in local politics, and at these elections their supporters either had to vote for nonpartisan lists or joint bourgeois lists. Since the beginning of the present century, local politics has become gradually more politicized. During the last three decades, it has become usual for a party to run lists in most of the communes (Norway, Central Bureau of Election Statistics; Rokkan and Valen, 1962; Hjellum, 1967).

The history of Labor, the third oldest party, is quite different. At the time it was formed (1887), it was a tiny group without much hope of obtaining parliamentary representation in the short run. A large part of its potential supporters could not even vote. Membership in a mass organization was a way for the disenfranchised to participate in the national decision-making process indirectly.

Labor has always emphasized strong and active organization. From the very beginning, local politics was a major target. Like other social democratic parties, Labor was surrounded by a number of auxiliary organizations, e.g., travel bureaus, insurance agencies, resorts, newspapers. The philosophy has been that representatives in public office should emerge from the party's organizations, "the movement." Moreover, the electoral organization should participate in the governmental process and—at least to some extent—have control over the elected representatives, both in local and national politics.

Thus, originally, the three oldest parties in Norway had considerable resemblance to the Duverger party model, but over the years the parties learned from one another. Duverger speaks of the "contamination from the left," suggesting that caucus parties, in order to compete effectively at elections, have to adopt some of the organizational features of mass parties. It is evident that the bourgeois parties in Norway, faced with competition from the dominant Labor Party, have strengthened their organizations considerably. Organizationally, all the major parties today are fairly similar. Experiments with alternative models have largely failed, such as a grass-roots model tried by the Socialist Left Party and a rudimentary mass movement model tried by the Progress Party (Svåsand, 1994: 306 ff.).

Party Membership

Norwegian political parties are membership organizations. Voters can join the party of their choice by registering with the party and paying modest dues.[6] Until 1992, the Labor Party had indirect members as well: local trade unions could affiliate with local labor parties and all the unions' members (save those who explicitly opted out) became individual members of the Labor Party. Norwegian parties are very open and permeable organizations.

Party members tend to be hard-core partisans. Only they can take part in the internal affairs of the parties—the selection of officials, the drafting of platforms, and the nomination of candidates to the Storting and to provincial and local offices. With few exceptions, conventions of party members monopolize access to public offices.

About 15 percent of the electorate are dues-paying party members. This overall figure has declined somewhat in recent decades. And, on the individual level, there is considerable turnover that is masked by the relative stability of the aggregate membership. The size of the various parties' memberships varies over time. The Labor Party since the 1960s has suffered a substantial decline in membership along with a decline in its vote share. Center Party membership has also suffered a long-term decline in the wake of a shrinking farm population, but the party tends to recover members as well as voters whenever EC becomes a salient issue. The Conservative Party's long-term decline in membership was reversed when conservative ideas became popular in the 1970s and 80s. Some of the losses by the older parties were made up by the new post–World War II parties, although neither the Socialist Left nor the Progress Party are particularly strong as membership organizations (Svåsand, 1994).

Belonging to a political party may be a necessary condition to becoming a political activist, but not all party members are active. A 1983 survey that compared the activity level of various organizations found that only 10 percent of party members were active by their definition (Svåsand, 1994: 317). Only trade unions and housing cooperatives had equally low rates of participation. This combination of openness and limited activism by party members becomes especially important in understanding the nominating process in Norway (see chapter 5).

The Party Hierarchy

The Norwegian parties are organized parallel to the government structure—they have branches at the local, provincial, and national levels that are primarily concerned with campaigns and elections at their respective levels. In principle, power and authority flow upward from the members in local branches (*partilag*), to the provincial (*fylke*) branches, to the national party. The national congress (*landsmote*) is the highest authority of the party and consists of delegates elected by provincial congresses, which in turn are elected at local meetings. Every other year (some parties do this every year), the national congress elects the national party leader (*partileder* or *partiformann*) and (usually) two deputy leaders (*nestleder* or *viseformann*). Party congresses debate policies and formulate the party's manifesto, and decide organizational matters. All these issues have been debated, of course, in the process of selecting delegates to the provincial and national congresses (see the description in Valen and Katz, 1964).

In between national congresses, the parties are run by two bodies elected by the congress. The first is a large national committee (*landsstyre*) that consists of representatives from all the provinces and auxiliary party organizations for women, youth, party employees, and so on. The landsstyre, which meets infrequently, has a smaller executive committee (*sentralstyre*), and some parties have an even smaller working committee (*arbeidsutvalg*) to run the party on a day-to-day basis.

While the organization charts suggest that the Norwegian parties are governed bottom up rather than top down, and while resistance to centralized power is a cherished tradition in Norway, there are important factors that work toward party centralization (Svåsand, 1994: 58 ff.). Part-time amateurs are no match for the full-time professional politicians one finds at the top of Norwegian parties. The mass media of communications give national leaders an opportunity to communicate directly with voters, bypassing the provincial and local party leaders. However, the strong local media tend to strengthen the lower echelons of these organizations. The technology of modern politics—polling, computer-targeted mass mailings, television, and so on—may have centralizing consequences if for no other reason than their great expense. But the power balance between the party membership and their leaders is not that clear or constant. The Labor Party under Einar Gerhardson probably was more centralized than the party under Gro Harlem Brundtland. A similar tendency may be observed within the Conservative Party, but the Progress Party has become more centralized in recent years (Svåsand, 1994).

In Norway, the mass party of Duverger, with its hierarchy and mass membership, won out over the bourgeois caucus parties. But mass membership of the Norwegian parties is shrinking. Perhaps the parties are moving toward a new stage, more like the old caucus party than a mass party in their organization and style. Could the contagion from the Left have been superseded by a contagion from the Right?

The Parliamentary Party

Parties represented in the Storting all have parliamentary party organizations distinct from but linked to the party organization outside. The party organization in the Storting is called the Storting's group (*Stortingsgruppe*), which is headed by a parliamentary leader elected by the group (*parlamentarisk fører*). Sometimes the positions of party parliamentary leaders and national leaders are held by the same person. In either event, the parliamentary leader is the main spokesperson for the party in the legislature and is a central figure in all inter-party negotiations (which are especially crucial under minority governments). The parlamentarisk fører usually serves in that position for several terms, becoming nationally prominent and a potential prime minister if he or she was not already one. The Conservative Party is a conspicuous exception to this trend; in recent decades their parliamentary leaders have had short and turbulent tenures.

In principle, the parliamentary party and its members are bound by the decisions of the national party. But the relationship is a bit more complicated than this implies. The electoral wing of the socialist parties have had the most control over their Stortingsgruppe, but the overlap of personnel—the party leader is usually also the parliamentary leader—reduces conflict and facilitates coordination. The Conservative Party, however, had tended not to combine the two top leadership positions, and the parliamentary leader was dominant until recent years. The Liberal Party was temporarily split by bickering between the parliamentary and electoral organizations over the EC issue. The Progress Party has recently changed its rules to make the national electoral party totally dominant over its parliamentarians. The relationship between the national party and the parliamentary party thus varies between parties and over time.

Party Finance

The political parties in Norway, as in most other modern countries, have become more professionalized in recent decades. This can mean different things to different people within different parties, but invariably professionalization requires full-time staffs at all levels of the party. This results in greater efficiency, expertise, and continuity, but at greater cost. Modern campaign techniques may be more effective than the old-time ways, but they are also more expensive. The traditional sources of party income—member dues, contributions by individuals and groups, and money-raising activities such as lotteries—were not adequate to support the kind of parties the political activists wanted. Thus in 1970, the Storting first provided for a public subsidy for political parties polling more than 1 percent of the vote in the previous election.[7] Today, these public funds are the most important source of income for all the major parties.

In 1970, the parties received 3.7 kroner per vote from the public treasury; now it is 22.1 kroner per vote (Svåsand, 1994: 321, table 12.1). These funds are allocated by a formula that is tilted toward the national level. Support for the parliamentary party is a separate budget item, as are subsidies to the party press and the parties' extensive educational associations. Today, "Norwegian parties have become almost totally dependent on the state for their existence" (Svåsand, 1994: 320).

This approach has important advantages. Neither the party nor the party candidates are required to devote time or energy to raising money. The potential political power of individual or organizational wealth is reduced if not entirely eliminated. The recruitment of candidates for elective office can proceed without thought of their personal wealth or access to other people's money. Most observers agree that the parties have become stronger and more effective organizations since 1970. And all the parties save for the right-wing Progress Party favor public subsidies, although they sometimes disagree over allocation formulas and other details.

There is a downside. If the requirements to qualify for public funding are set very low, the public finance system encourages the founding of new parties; if the qualifying figures are high, they discourage new entrants into the political game. Fund raising traditionally has been an important task for party activists. It is possible that public funding has contributed to the decline in party activism, although the experts are of two minds on this point.

Voluntary Associations

Norway is one of the most thoroughly organized societies in the world. The beginnings of this pattern can be traced back at least to the early nineteenth century (Kvavik, 1976). Most of the earliest voluntary associations were local, established for cultural or humanitarian purposes. Examples of such groups (all eventually became nationwide organizations) are the Norwegian Bible Society, the Society for the Protection of Norwegian Antiquities, the Norwegian Sports Union, and the Norwegian Temperance Association. As the century progressed, the numbers of voluntary associations continued to grow and their focus shifted more toward occupational and economic concerns (fig. 2.1). Note that the most rapid growth of associations was from about 1945 to 1960—the period when the welfare state developed.

A few associations have formal relationships with the political parties. When the Labor Party was founded in 1887, it served both as a political party and a trade union. This marriage of convenience was broken up in 1899 when the Norwegian Federation of Trade Unions (LO) was established as a separate organization. But a cordial relationship has always existed between the two. Thus, until 1992 local unions could join the party collectively, and the unions have always supported the party financially. A

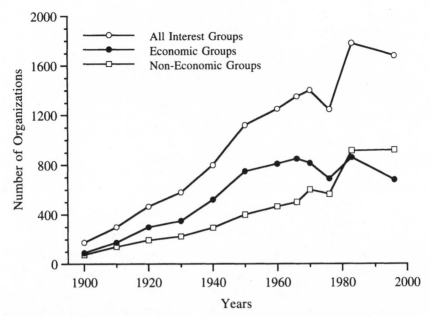

Figure 2.1 Growth of Organizations in Norway, 1900–1995. *Sources:* Kvavik (1976), graph 2.1; Norwegian Social Science Data Service, database on non-profit organizations.

cooperation committee between the party and LO exists on the national level, in which top leaders from the unions and the party meet regularly and often to discuss their common interests in current political issues.

A similar development is evident on the agrarian side. The main Farmers' Association (Norges Landmandsforbund) was founded in 1896; originally it tended to cooperate closely with the Liberal Party. But during the period 1906–18, the organization on several occasions ran separate lists at national elections. In 1920 the Agrarian Party was formed on the initiative of the Farmers' Association, and for the first few years the party and the interest organization existed in an organizational symbiosis. After they separated in the 1930s, the Farmers' Association emphasized its neutrality in relation to political parties, and in 1946 it adopted a rule that the organization would not grant money to any political party. The Federation of Employers' Organizations (founded 1900) has never been formally linked to any specific party, but it has tended to support the bourgeois parties financially, particularly the Conservatives. The newer political parties—Christians, Socialist Left, and Progress—have no formal connections with groups and associations.

Table 2.2

Governmental Boards Active in Selected Years

Years	Permanent Boards	Temporary Boards	All
1936	192	69	261
1951	378	125	503
1966	804	150	954
1971	838	231	1,069
1976	912	229	1,141
1980	920	172	1,092
1983	860	147	1,007
1986	804	94	898
1989	749	77	826

Source: Nordby (1994), 80, table 2.

The vast majority of all voluntary associations in Norway are thus officially nonpartisan—even when there is a significant membership overlap with one of the parties. This does not mean that these associations are politically insignificant. Rather, most associations in Norway prefer other ways to influence public policy. Connecting with a political party risks isolation from centers of decision if that political party loses. The political interests of most organizations are too narrow for political parties to adopt without substantial modification (viewed as watering down by the organizations' true believers).

The larger and more powerful associations in Norway are in regular contact with the government through the network of commissions, councils, committees, advising boards, steering boards, conferences, and so on that Norwegian politicians and civil servants find useful. The private organizations, of course, tend to welcome regular involvement in the policy-making process, too. There are risks for both sides in this mode of formulating and implementing policy (see Olsen, 1983: chap. 5). But the benefits seem greater to most Norwegians. Neo-corporatism is a major attribute of Norwegian political life.

A few figures will illustrate this point. Table 2.2 shows the number of governmental boards or commissions (both permanent and temporary) that were active in selected years since 1936. Note the rapid growth in the postwar period to a high of 1,141 active boards in 1976. There has been some decline since to 800–900 governmental commissions. The proportion of these commissions that contain members drawn from interest organizations has increased over the years. In 1936, 25 percent of the permanent boards and 48 percent of the temporary boards contained participants from interest organizations; in 1989 the comparable figures were 51 percent and 64 percent (Nordby, 1994: 79, table 1). This means, of course, that the larger interest organizations are represented on many of these governmental boards. In 1957, for example, LO was represented on forty-nine boards and the Norwegian Industrial Association on forty-two. Even the Organization for Sports Fishing provided members for seventeen governmental boards (Heidar, 1983: 232, table 7.4).

Thus, voluntary associations are a significant part of the political landscape in Norway. They play important representational roles, most of which we will not be able to examine in a book on the Storting. But not all organizations or interests can be represented in neo-corporatist arrangements with the state. Those persons and groups not included in these public-private collaborations have another place to turn—the Storting.

Consensus Democracy

In his important book on political democracy, Arend Lijphart (1984) develops a very useful typology of democratic regimes. The first type, the Westminster model, is based on the principle of majority rule. Nations belonging to this category have two-party systems and plurality elections. The party that wins an election forms a government that dominates the parliament. The second type of democracy, the consensus model, "tries to maximize the size of the ruling majority instead of being satisfied with a bare majority." These regimes tend toward multiparty systems and proportional representation (PR). The essence of the consensus model is the inclusion of opposition parties in the governing process (see also Elder, Thomas, and Arter, 1982).

Most countries do not fit either of these models perfectly. But these types can be thought of as polar opposites, while real-life political systems are located along a continuum between the two. Norway fits well toward the consensus end of the continuum. It is a multiparty state, with multidimensional conflict and proportional representation. No single party has held a majority of the seats in the Storting since 1961, and it seems unlikely that any party will in the foreseeable future. The governments are either multiparty coalitions or minority governments. Both types of governments require the collaboration of two or more parties in order to win the majority votes in the Storting required to govern. Multiparty coalitions—which require public and formal agreements between parties and a sharing of cabinet seats—are far less common in Norway than minority governments. Either way, collaboration across party lines is a fact of life.

The reluctance of Norwegian political parties to join governing coalitions results from the fact that parties not in a government retain substantial influence on policy while avoiding the risks of becoming part of a government (Strøm, 1990). Governing parties in Norway tend to lose electoral support, even though the tendency is most evident for parties competing along the left-right axis (Strøm, 1990; Narud, 1996a). Ironically, in the Norwegian case, governments with minority electoral bases may be more inclusive in their policy-making than majority governments (Strøm, 1990). Minority governments strengthen the Storting as an institution, since it is in Storting committees that the final stages of consensus creation usually occurs.

Consensus democracy has consequences for political representation. Strict accountability through the parties is sacrificed: by the time a new policy is made, so many groups and parties have contributed to it that it is difficult to pinpoint praise or blame. It can be very slow in arriving at decisions. But policies once adopted have broad support that (arguably) makes for more legitimacy, less conflict, fewer policy U-turns, and easier policy implementation than in more majoritarian systems. It is difficult to overestimate the significance of the consensus style of Norwegian democracy.

3

The Electoral System

"O ne man, one vote!" was a clarion call of nineteenth-century political reform. Despite its near universal appeal, the principle has proven difficult to achieve in practice. At first, huge categories of people were exempt from its strictures—women, slaves, serfs, poor people, the young. As these groups gradually achieved full citizenship, other problems became apparent. The way elections were conducted turned out to have consequences—sometimes major consequences.[1] For example, plurality electoral systems based on single-member districts (as in Britain and the United States) stress territorial equity. The strength of the political parties can be distorted in the process of converting popular votes into legislative seats. In electoral systems with proportional representation, as in most European democracies, the division of the vote between parties is closely mirrored in the distribution of seats in the legislature, but the various regions and districts within the country may be over- or underrepresented. Equity for one set of people disadvantages others. The idea that everyone's vote should carry equal weight—implicit in the "one man, one vote" ideal—is elusive in practice.

In this chapter we describe how Norwegians have struggled with these intractable problems, beginning with the constitution of 1814. And we shall point out how their solutions have affected political representation in Norway.

Toward a Democratic Electoral System

The electoral system specified in the Constitution of 1814 reflected the ideas of its time. The right to vote was given to men at least twenty-five years of age who were government officials, registered burghers, or free-holding farmers. This group (small by contemporary standards but large for the early 1800s) was permitted to vote for delegates to an electoral college (*valgmannsmote*) held in each constituency. Secret voting was not required. The valgmannsmote then selected the representatives to the Storting. These arrangements worked agreeably well throughout most of the nineteenth century, although they came under increasing attack toward the end. The requirements to qualify for voting were made less stringent in 1884 and the secret ballot guaranteed. In 1898 universal manhood suffrage was achieved—although women had to wait until 1913 for the vote. (In 1907, women with a specified minimum annual income, or married to men with that income, were permitted to vote in national elections.)

The last early nineteenth-century idea to be abandoned was the indirect election of members of the Storting. Not only was the practice undemocratic and insulting, the reformers argued, but it often resulted in the election of unrepresentative Storting members. The application of the majority rule principle at both the election stage and the subsequent constituency electoral college sometimes had undesirable consequences. Bjørn Kristvik and Stein Rokkan (1964: 6) provide an example from a small urban constituency in Finnmark at the 1897 Storting election. The votes were distributed as follows:

	Right		Left	
		Electoral College		Electoral College
Towns	Voters	Delegates	Voters	Delegates
Hammerfest	648	5	501	0
Vardo	926	0	1,892	8
Vadso	954	6	748	0
Total	2,528	11	3,141	8

Although the Left polled a large majority in this constituency, the Right won a majority in the electoral college and hence the single Storting seat. This was not a unique case (Kristvik and Rokkan 1964: 34). Such blatantly unfair outcomes contributed to a decision by the Storting in 1905 to replace the old system with direct popular elections. With that decision, Norway entered a new and more democratic era in electoral politics.

The coming of democracy to Norway, as elsewhere, required that a small enfranchised elite decide (voluntarily or otherwise) to share its power with the previously voteless masses. This occurred in part because of the spread throughout the West of powerful democratic ideas that implied universal suffrage, secret and direct election, equality of representation, and so on. But practical politics played a part, too. Factional conflict between the left and the right in the Storting became more frequent and structured in the late nineteenth century, hardening into recognizable political parties by 1884. The Left Party stood to gain strength by broadening the franchise to include more ordinary Norwegians. The Right, while less enthusiastic about democracy and equality than its liberal colleagues and realizing that this reform would disadvantage it, still was not willing to risk social disorder in order to defend the status quo.[2]

Nineteenth-Century Principles and Modern Elections

Three principles established by the constitutional assembly of 1814 have affected the electoral system and its workings to the present day. First, the basic principles of the system, including the definition of constituencies and the number of seats assigned to each constituency, were specified in the Constitution. Since constitutional amendments require a two-thirds majority vote in the Storting, it is difficult to change electoral arrangements.

The wisdom of this decision is arguable. One of the inescapable consequences of elections is that they create both winners and losers, whose reactions to election results are predictably different. John Kingdon (1966) points out this "congratulation-rationalization" effect. Winners tend to ascribe their victory to their own stellar qualities; losers tend to blame their loss on uncontrollable factors—usually "the system." Small wonder that proposals to reform the electoral system are always with us! The authors of the Constitution of 1814 wanted to guard against frequent or frivolous fiddling with the electoral system—a laudable goal. But in achieving that objective they may have made it too difficult to revise Norwegian electoral arrangements to keep up with a rapidly changing world. No matter how one evaluates this trade-off, the constitutional status of much of Norwegian electoral law is an important fact today.

The second decision of the constitutional assembly of 1814, which still shapes political representation, was to over-represent the peripheral regions as compared to central areas. While Norway is a small country in terms of population, this population is scattered over a large area with a profusion of fjords, mountains, forests, and other barriers to transportation and communications. The various regions and communities in Norway developed in relative isolation from one another for many generations; the predictable results are geographically based differences in values, customs, language—and politics (see Rokkan, 1970). To many Norwegians the region around what is now called Oslo is viewed in much the same way that New York City is seen by many Americans—as an essentially foreign place where untrustworthy strangers dwell. The Electoral Reform Commission of 1917 provided a more polite justification for under-representing Oslo in its report: "Although the commission shares the opinion that it would be desirable to allocate more seats to Kristiania [Oslo], the perception is that this city as the capital has access to political and parliamentarian influence which cannot be neglected. As the seat of the most important newspapers in the country, of all political parties, of economic and professional organizations, and of central financial and administrative institutions, the capital holds a particular position implying that it cannot to the same extent as other constituencies demand representation proportional to the size of its population or its electorate" (Norway, *Valgordningskommisjonen av 1917*). Some of the same thinking led to the creation of a voteless District of Columbia as the home place for the U.S. federal government. The intentional under-representation of Norway's Southeast has contributed to the maintenance and reinforcement of territorial cleavage between the center and the periphery of the country. (See Rokkan and Valen, 1964; Rokkan, 1970; Valen and Rokkan, 1974.)

The third constitutional principle that has shaped modern Norwegian politics was the decision that urban and rural areas should vote separately, with seats allocated in a ratio of one urban seat in the Storting for every two rural seats. Officially this "farmers' paragraph" was written into the Constitution to protect the countryside. In reality, however, it greatly favored urban areas, which claimed only about one-fifth of the total population in 1814.[3] This changed significantly as the country became more urban in the wake of industrialism. But the farmers' paragraph remained controversial until it was abandoned in 1953.

From Majority Rule to PR

When the Storting decided in 1905 to replace the old system with direct, majority elections, it was expected that the new system would create more proportionality between partisan vote distributions and allocation of seats (Kristvik and Rokkan, 1964; Norway, *Instilling fra Valgordningskommisjonen av 1900*, 17). The debates in the Storting also revealed that a vocal majority wanted to strengthen direct contacts between voters and representatives and to make the individual candidates more visible. Apparently, this was an important reason why majority elections in single-member constituencies were preferred to some form of proportional representation. It is less clear why the continental type of majority elections (with run-off elections) was preferred to the plurality system, as in Britain and the U.S. It is important to keep in mind, however, that the reform was introduced in an atmosphere of national conciliation due to the struggle with Sweden over the union. In this situation party differences were minimal except for the rapidly growing Labor Party, which differed from the others. Several bourgeois leaders advocated abolishing the parties and preferred an electoral system favoring cooperation among bourgeois parties (Kristvik, 1953; Kristvik and Rokkan, 1964; Christophersen, 1976).

After the breakup of the union, old party differences soon reappeared. Under the new electoral system, the two large parties on the bourgeois side tended to cooperate in the run-off elections. Thus, the election of 1918 gave the following results:

	Right	Left	Farmers Organization	Labor
Rural constituencies				
% votes	21.1	42.4	6.6	29.9
% seats	21.4	63.1	3.6	11.9
Urban constituencies				
% votes	49.9	14.9	—	35.2
% seats	78.6	2.4	—	19.0

The main loser was the growing Labor Party. The party's under-representation increased almost regularly from election to election. This happened in a period when Labor was in a process of radicalization (see chap. 2). The party demanded the introduction of proportional representation and threatened a boycott of future elections. The bourgeois parties realized that reform was unavoidable: the Labor Party would continue to grow. In the event that Labor became a majority party in the Storting, the Left and Right parties would have little influence. Proportional representation—a system that promises a close correspondence between the distribution of votes and seats—would make it more difficult for Labor to achieve majority status in the Storting and assure the middle-class parties of a place in the Storting roughly equivalent to their numbers in the electorate. PR was a prudent compromise (Kristvik and Rokkan, 1964).

Thus, in 1919, the majority election system was replaced by PR. As will be demonstrated in the next section, the new system, which applied the d'Hondt formula of representation, tended to over-represent the larger parties. In an attempt to adjust for this, a system of electoral alliances (*Listeforbund*) was introduced in 1930.[4] At subsequent elections the bourgeois parties, by applying the Listeforbund, gained a number of extra seats at the expense of the dominant Labor Party. In 1949, when Labor held a majority position in the Storting, the Listeforbund was removed.

In 1953 the political parties agreed on a major reform to improve proportionality between vote and seat distributions. For one thing, the distinction between urban and rural representation, i.e., the farmers' paragraph, was removed from the Constitution. From now on, urban and rural communities of each province would constitute a joint constituency. Oslo and Bergen were the only pure urban constituencies left.[5] Second, some adjustments were obtained in seat allocations for individual provinces. Third, the d'Hondt formula of representation was replaced by a modified version of the Sainte Laguë formula. This reform improved equity of representation.[6]

In 1985 the bourgeois majority in the Storting voted in favor of reintroducing the system of Listeforbund, which greatly benefited the bourgeois parties in the subsequent election (Valen, 1994). This reform forced the Labor Party to accept in 1989 an old proposal for eight supplementary nationwide seats to balance the representation between parties. Supplementary seats allocated to parties that are under-represented are placed in provinces in which the respective parties have the highest quotients of unused votes. Only parties that have obtained at least 4 percent of the national vote are entitled to have a share of the supplementary seats.[7] As part of the reform, the Listeforbund was removed and prohibited for the future by a constitutional amendment.

From Votes to Seats

Now that we have described the changing electoral system of Norway, we turn our attention to measuring its effects on representation. In this section we will focus on how the electoral system impacts the representation of political parties in the Storting. In the next section we will examine the electoral system's effects on the distribution of seats among the provinces (*fylker*), and in the final section we show the combined effects on both.

Throughout the following analysis we shall use a new concept—ideal

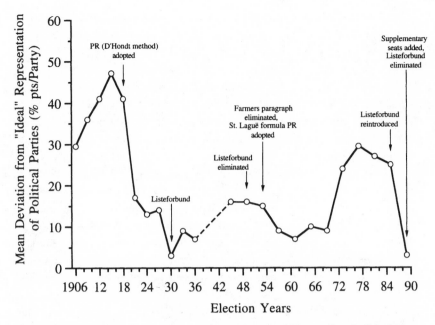

Figure 3.1 Deviations from Ideal Representation of Norwegian Political Parties, 1906–1989

representation. Ideal representation is the situation when the proportion of votes cast and the proportion of seats awarded are exactly the same, as in:

$$\frac{\% \text{ of seats}}{\% \text{ of votes}} = 1$$

In this situation the electoral system has converted popular votes in parliamentary seats without any error (or deviation, or bias—words we shall use interchangeably). A more typical case could look like this: Party A received 35 percent of the popular vote but won 40 percent of the seats: $40\% \div 35\% = 1.14$. This means that Party A has received 14 percent more seats in the parliament than ideal. That difference results from the workings of the electoral system. Of course, parties are not always so fortunate as Party A. Party B polled 20 percent of the popular vote but won only 10 percent of the seats, or: $10\% \div 20\% = 0.50$. Party B has won only half its ideal number of seats, hence the error $(1.0 - 0.50)$ is 50 percent.

Using this approach, figure 3.1 indicates how closely the Norwegian electoral system has come to representing the preferences of Norwegian voters for the various political parties since direct popular elections were begun in 1906. The figure displays the average (or mean) deviation from the ideal seats/votes ratio of the major political parties.[8] Thus, in 1906, the average political party received 29.7 percent more, or fewer, seats in the Storting than its votes would have won in an ideal electoral system (i.e., one without error). Note how the single-member district electoral system continued to make very large average errors—between 30 percent and 50 percent—until PR was introduced in 1919. Then the average error plummeted. The addition of Listeforbund permitting electoral alliances between parties resulted in the elections immediately prior to World War II being exceedingly accurate in translating votes into seats, so far as the parties were concerned. After the re-establishment of normal politics in 1945, the electoral system performed nearly as well, especially after the major reforms of 1952. In the 1970s, however, the average party's deviation from the ideal increased sharply to between 20 percent and 30 percent before recent reforms seem to have reduced the errors sharply once again.

What accounts for these fluctuations? Changes in the electoral law have been one apparent cause. But the changes seem to have temporary effects—the initial reduction in error after an electoral reform seems short-lived. A look at deviation from the ideal on a party-by-party basis suggests still other factors (see table 3.1). At first Høyre and Venstre, the two original and largest parties, benefited and the Labor Party suffered from the electoral arrangements. Even after the introduction of PR in 1921 it took several national elections before the Labor Party began to have a seats/votes ratio over 1.0, and by then it was the largest political party in the country. From 1927 into the '90s, the Labor Party has been the main beneficiary of the electoral systems' inexactitudes. All new and small parties, with the exception of the Farmers'/Center Party, have had a hard time getting started; all the electoral arrangements used in Norway since 1906 have tended to favor the strong. In table 3.2 we compare the percentage of the ideal number of seats the political parties won to the percentage of the vote they received. During the single-member district period (1906–18), parties polling more than 40 percent of the vote received 137 percent of their ideal number of seats and all smaller parties received less than their ideal share. This distortion has been drastically reduced by the introduction of PR, although large- and medium-sized political parties remain advantaged as compared to small parties. The accuracy of the Norwegian electoral systems in assigning seats to parties seems greatest in times of partisan stability (the 1950s and '60s) and most prone to error in times of rapid party change (immediately after World

Table 3.1
Ideal Representation of Political Parties

Year	H	V	DNA	BP/SP	KrF	SV	FrP	All Others	Mean Error (in %)
1906	87	131	55	—	—	—	—	66	29.7
1909	126	122	42	—	—	—	—	4	35.3
1912	59	154	72	—	—	—	—	—	41.0
1915	59	180	47	—	—	—	—	117	47.7
1918	127	146	45	—	—	—	—	58	40.6
1921	114	125	89	—	—	—	—	72	16.7
1924	111	122	87	108	—	—	—	66	13.5
1927	83	116	107	116	—	—	—	46	14.0
1930	102	105	100	105	—	—	—	46	3.0
1933	99	94	115	110	12	—	—	25	8.8
1936	113	96	110	103	93	—	—	1	7.4
1945	98	96	123	83	67	—	—	60	15.8
1949	98	96	124	86	63	—	—	60	16.2
1953	97	100	109	99	86	—	—	39	15.4
1957	102	103	109	108	78	—	—	17	8.6
1961	96	106	105	115	104	—	—	24	6.8
1965	98	115	105	121	107	—	—	18	10.0
1969	98	91	106	127	99	—	—	0	9.0
1973	107	37	113	124	106	92	52	0	24.1
1977	107	41	116	90	115	31	0	0	29.3
1981	108	33	115	108	103	53	58	0	27.1
1985	105	0	111	115	123	69	35	0	25.0
1989	101	0	111	103	102	102	102	< 1	3.5
1993	100	17	110	119	100	100	95	55	20.3

Notes: Ideal representation is % Seats ÷ % Votes = 1.

Mean error is arithmetic sum of deviations from 100 percent for major parties divided by the number of parties. All other parties omitted from the means. Venstre omitted from means in 1985 and 1989.

War II and the '70s and early '80s). The emergence of new parties and the rapid decline of old ones leads to growing errors in partisan representation. Under these conditions, one or two parties each poll around 35 percent of the vote (and hence are awarded more than their proportionate share of seats) while the other parties remain small (and hence are underrepresented in the Storting). When, however, all the parties in the system are nearly the same size, distortions of partisan representation are reduced.

Table 3.2

Seats Won by Parties, by % of Vote Received (In Average % of Ideal Number of Seats)

% Vote Received by Parties	1906–18 (Single-Member Districts)	1921–49 (PR, d'Hondt)	1953–69 (PR, St. Laguë)	1973–85	1989
40–49	137	118	107	113	—
30–39	99	108	—	110	111
20–29	74	97	97	107	101
10–19	—	89	94	111	102
0–9	59	51	75	47	1

Note: The entries are the average percent of the ideal seat distribution a party receives for a given level of voter support. The 1989 figures are for a single election; more elections are needed to have confidence in them.

Territorial Representation

The election of parliamentarians from geographical districts, rather than from the country at large, introduces a second possible source of distortion in the process of representation.

In Norway, the single-member district electoral system resulted in almost as large departures from ideal representation as vote counting rules (see figure 3.2). In 1906 the average province received 27.5 percent more (or fewer) seats in the Storting than its proportionate share. This divergence from an ideal apportionment of seats increased until in 1918 the average divergence from the ideal was 35 percentage points. As the nation industrialized and urbanized, the constitutional definition of the electoral districts and assignment of seats and the farmers' paragraph led to increasing differences in the size of the electoral districts and in the voting power of individual Norwegians. This clashed with the people's growing commitment to democratic and egalitarian values.

There were several possible solutions to this problem. One approach might have been to abandon reliance on long-standing political units—the fylker—as electoral units and to redraw electoral district lines periodically to account for changes in population growth and distribution. This is how single-member electoral districts are kept approximately equal in size for the U.S. House of Representatives. This approach results in artificial and changing electoral districts with boundaries that often do not coincide with those of other political units. Redrawing the boundaries of

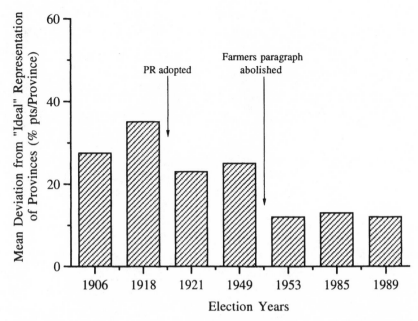

Figure 3.2 Deviations from Ideal Representation of Norwegian Provinces, Selected Years

such electoral units is difficult, fraught with danger of partisan manipulation, and usually inelegant to behold. The fylker were more than convenient administrative entities; they were, in varying degrees, real political communities with well-established natural boundaries and histories and traditions that inspired loyalty. Their centrality to the electoral system was embedded in a Constitution praised with fervor (and more than a little *Aquavit*) every 17th of May. The Norwegians thus decided to keep the fylker as the primary electoral units, but to add additional seats to the larger ones, and to choose Storting members within the fylker by proportional representation.

The result of this change was a reduction in the average deviation from ideal representation of the provinces to the 20–25 percent range. The abandonment of the farmers' paragraph along with the changes passed in 1952 has cut that average error to the 12–15 percent range. This is about half the amount of error we found during the same period in assigning seats to political parties.

The attentive reader should not be surprised to learn that these departures from ideal representation are not randomly distributed (see table 3.3). Oslo and its immediate environs are heavily under-represented,

Table 3.3
% of Ideal Representation Received by Fylke

Province	1906	1918	1921	1949	1953	1985	1989	1993
Østfold	109	112	117	100	89	89	95	87
Akershus	71	53	68	82	78	83	94	83
Oslo	39	31	38	30	55	79	87	91
Hedmark	85	84	105	99	99	112	106	107
Oppland	76	81	88	111	97	101	96	96
Buskerud	95	89	94	103	91	84	79	90
Vestfold	126	118	120	108	92	96	90	89
Telemark	143	152	134	122	92	96	93	127
Aust-Agder	169	164	126	201	120	115	108	108
Vest-Agder	170	183	137	113	115	98	93	70
Rogaland	123	114	113	117	106	88	98	84
Hordaland	95	112	107	97	122	101	102	94
Bergen	84	69	79	88	91	a	a	a
Sogn og Fjordane	97	176	103	116	124	126	122	123
Møre og Romsdal	92	127	105	122	122	113	108	111
Sør-Trøndelag	115	112	109	121	110	106	101	102
Nord-Trøndelag	89	95	102	107	129	126	121	123
Nordland	118	114	113	110	149	131	126	138
Troms	107	146	168	169	142	109	104	111
Finnmark	193	174	200	183	167	143	139	155
All Norway	100	100	100	100	100	100	100	100
Mean Error	27.5	34.9	22.8	24.8	12.1	12.7	11.7	16.9

aCombined with Hordaland.

although this penalty for being close to the center of power has been reduced since the early twentieth century. The nation's second-largest city,
Bergen, was also under-represented until it was merged with the province
that surrounds it (Hordaland). The rural eastern fylker have—since the
abandonment of single-member districts and the farmers' paragraph—
done less well than the rural West and North. Basically, the entire nation
north of Bergen is over-represented (with the two fylker containing significant cities, Sør-Trøndelag and Troms, being partial exceptions).

An "Ideal" Storting

Comparing actual election results with a hypothetical ideal has allowed
us to look at two different sources of error in representation: the apportionment of seats to provinces and the conversion of party votes to party
seats within the provinces. These two distortions can reinforce one another (as when a party gets more than its ideal share of the seats in an
over-represented province) or have contradictory and self-canceling effects (as when a party gets more than its share of the seats in an under-
represented area).

A way of getting at the combined impact of both sources of error is to
construct a hypothetical ideal Storting in which each seat represents exactly the same number of people ($\frac{1}{157}$ of the enfranchised population in
1985) and where the percentage of seats each party wins within each province is exactly the same as its percentage of the vote. Multiply the percentage of seats won by parties times the ideal number of seats each province
should have, add the results to get the national totals, and then round to
the nearest whole number. Presto! An "ideally" representative Storting!

Table 3.4 displays the ideal number of Storting seats each province
should have had in recent elections and compares that with the actual
number of seats each possessed. Only seven provinces in 1985 and eight
in 1989 were exactly on the mark; all the others gained or lost at least one
seat. The by-now familiar under-representation of Oslo and the Southeast, and over-representation of the North and West, is apparent. The
Labor and Conservative parties, which dominate in both areas, lost several seats in the Southeast because the region was under-represented but
more than made up for that in the North, which has a good many more
seats than the ideal. The addition of supplementary seats in 1989—all of
them went to urban fylker, mostly in the East—reduced geographical
distortion in representation noticeably. But at the subsequent election

Table 3.4

Actual Number of Seats Assigned to Provinces Compared to Ideal Number

Province	1985			1989			1993		
	Ideal No. of Seats	Actual No.	Difference	Ideal No. of Seats	Actual No.	Difference	Ideal No. of Seats	Actual No.	Difference
Østfold	9	8	−1	10	9	−1	9	8	−1
Akershus	15	12	−3	16	15	−1	17	14	−3
Oslo	18	15	−3	18	16	−2	19	17	−2
Hedmark	7	8	+1	8	8	0	7	8	+1
Oppland	7	7	0	7	7	0	7	7	0
Buskerud	8	7	−1	9	7	−2	9	8	−1
Vestfold	7	7	0	8	7	−1	8	7	−1
Telemark	6	6	0	6	6	0	6	8	+2
Aust-Agder	4	4	0	4	4	0	4	4	0
Vest-Agder	5	5	0	5	5	0	5	5	0
Rogaland	11	10	−1	12	12	0	13	11	−2
Hordaland	15	15	0	16	16	0	16	15	−1
Sogn og Fjordane	4	5	+1	4	5	+1	4	5	+1
Møre og Romsdal	9	10	+1	9	10	+1	9	10	+1
Sør-Trøndelag	9	10	+1	9	10	+1	9	10	+1
Nord-Trøndelag	5	6	+1	5	6	+1	5	6	+1
Nordland	9	12	+3	9	12	+3	9	12	+3
Troms	6	6	0	6	6	0	5	6	+1
Finnmark	3	4	+1	3	4	+1	3	4	+1

distortion increased once more because of a new distribution of the supplementary seats.

In table 3.5 we see the Storting partisan division in recent elections—both ideal and actual. The workings of the electoral system increased the Labor Party's ranks from sixty-four to seventy-one in 1985. The Conservatives gained two seats, the Christians three, the Center Party two. All the other parties earned fewer seats than their numbers would justify in a perfectly representative national legislature. In 1989, the partisan distortions of the electoral system were reduced, but Labor still gained six seats and the Conservatives and Progress Party one seat each. Ironically, it was the Liberals—the party that benefited most from the electoral system during the early 1900s—that was hardest hit. Having polled enough votes nationwide to elect five members to the Storting in both election years, they received no seats at all. At the 1993 election the Liberals had a comeback in the Storting in that they won one seat in the province of Hordaland. At the same time a new party, the Red Electoral Alliance (Marxist-Leninists), unexpectedly obtained one seat in Oslo. Both parties had, however, less than 4 percent of the national vote, and consequently, they could not claim a share of the supplementary seats. The under-representation of these two mini-parties at the last election accounts for the increase of partisan distortion from 1989 to 1993.

Conclusions

In spite of numerous reforms, the electoral system of Norway has always resulted in some distortion of representation. The long-term trend over the last hundred years has been in favor of gradually more proportionality between vote distributions and seat allocations for individual parties. Nevertheless, territorial distortion has always been evident, with over-representation for peripheral regions. This over-representation was introduced in the Constitution of 1814 and has since been accepted as a necessary, or at least inevitable, element of the system. As a consequence, voters in peripheral areas carry more weight than do voters in central regions in the process of representation. Under-representation is most evident in constituencies with a high proportion of urban population.

The linkages between elected representatives and their voters have been greatly affected by these electoral reforms. The linkages must have been almost nonexistent during the period of indirect elections (1814–1905). With the introduction of majority elections in single-member

Table 3.5

Actual Number of Seats Won by Political Parties Compared to Ideal Seat Distribution (%)

Party	1985			1989			1993		
	Ideal No. of Seats	Actual No.	Difference	Ideal No. of Seats	Actual No.	Difference	Ideal No. of Seats	Actual No.	Difference
Labor	64	71	+7	57	63	+6	63	67	+4
Conservative	48	50	+2	36	37	+1	29	28	−1
Christian People's	13	16	+3	14	14	0	13	13	0
Center	10	12	+2	11	11	0	28	32	+4
Socialist Left	9	6	−3	17	17	0	13	13	0
Progress	6	2	−4	21	22	+1	11	10	−1
Liberal	5	0	−5	5	0	−5	6	1	−5
All others	2	0	−2	4	1	−3	2	1	−1

constituencies in 1905, a direct link was established between the representatives and their voters. At least within each territorial constituency, individual voters were now in a position to identify their own representatives. In 1919, when the PR system was introduced, this direct linkage disappeared. From then on the voters in the separate multimember constituencies had to relate to a collectivity of representatives. The introduction in 1989 of nationwide supplementary seats implies a further loosening of the representative's ties to the local constituency. Since these supplementary seats tend to fluctuate between the constituencies from one election to the next, supplementary representatives are likely to feel less committed to their current constituency than do the ordinary district representatives.

Despite all this, it would be a mistake to conclude that local interests go unrepresented in the Storting. Strong ties to a given constituency are normally required in order to be nominated by a political party (see chap. 5). Once elected, members of the Storting must win re-nomination every four years from provincial party conventions dominated by local politicians. As we shall see in chapter 9, serving the parochial interests of their constituencies is a preoccupation of many Storting members.

Appendix

Counting Votes by Two Different Systems of PR: An Example

The province of Hedmark had eight Storting seats in 1985. These are represented by the letters A, B, C, . . . H. Eleven party lists were on the ballot. In our example below, we confine our attention to the top seven lists. The Labor Party received the most votes, 71,924, and the other parties are arranged across the top row of the table in the order of the magnitude of the vote they each received (see table below).

Under the d'Hondt formula, the party with the most votes (Labor) automatically wins the first seat, "A." The total number of Labor votes is then divided by two, which is 35,962. This figure is compared to the total votes received by the other parties. Since no party received more votes than this, Labor receives the second seat, "B." The labor total is then divided by 3: the resulting 23,974 is still larger than the votes received by any other party, so Labor is awarded seat "C." Finally, when the total Labor vote is divided by 4, the resulting number is smaller (17,981) than the Conservative Party's total of 20,658 so the Conservatives win seat "D." The Conser-

Party	DNA	H	SP	SV	KrF	FrP	V
Total Votes	71,924	20,658	11,851	10,118	3,842	2,062	1,582

The d'Hondt Formula

Divided by							
1	71,924 (A)	20,658 (D)	11,851 (H)	10,118	3,842	2,062	1,582
2	35,962 (B)	10,329					
3	23,974 (C)						
4	17,981 (E)						
5	14,385 (F)						
6	11,987 (G)						
7	10,275						
Seats Won	6	1	1	0	0	0	0 = 8

The Modified Sainte Laguë Formula

Divided by							
1.4	51,374 (A)	14,756 (C)	8,465 (F)	7,227 (H)	2,744	1,473	1,130
3	23,975 (B)	6,866	3,950				
5	14,385 (D)						
7	10,275 (E)						
9	7,992 (G)						
11	6,539						
Seats Won	5	1	1	1	0	0	0 = 8

Notes: A, B, C . . . H represent the 8 seats to be filled.
Parties receiving less than 1,000 votes are not reported here.

vatives then have 10,329 votes remaining after dividing their total vote by 2. The Labor votes divided by 4 (resulting in 17,981), 5 (resulting in 14,385), and 6 (resulting in 11,987) are larger than the total votes of any of the other parties totals and the remaining 10,329 Conservative votes. Thus, the Labor Party is awarded seats "E," "F," and "G." Finally, when the Labor Party total vote is divided by 7 (resulting in 10,275) the Center

Party has more total votes than this and wins seat "H." The results then are Labor 6 seats, Conservatives 1 seat and Center party 1 seat.

Counting the same voting results with the modified Sainte Laguë formula proceeds in exactly the same way only the divisors are 1.4, 3, 5, 7, 9, and so on. As the table indicates, the results are also different: Labor 5 seats, Conservatives 1, Center Party 1, and Socialist Left 1 seat. The modified Sainte Laguë approach is more favorable to smaller parties than the d'Hondt formula.

4

The Storting

It stands upon a gentle rise looking down the boulevard toward the Kings Castle. In the midst of central Oslo, it is not as large, nor as replete with architectural flourishes, as the homes of most national legislatures. Its boxy, brick exterior is embellished by little save a generously bowed facade that contains the building's entryway. Inside, it is spacious, functional, nonheroic.

Of course, the Storting should not be confused with the building in which it resides.[1] The Storting is an institution—a set of rules about organization and procedure. In this chapter we shall present an introductory description of these rules and point out some of their consequences.

Organization and Procedures

The Storting is a unique combination of a unicameral and a bicameral parliament. It is unicameral in the sense that all representatives are elected in a single election, under identical suffrage requirements. Elections are held regularly every fourth year, and the Storting cannot be dissolved in the intervening period. The bicameral element results from the arrangement of the Storting into two divisions, Odelsting and Lagting, consisting of three-fourths and one-fourth of the assembly. After each election the political parties in the Storting decide how their members should be divided between them. The rule of proportionality among the parties is strictly observed in the composition of the two divisions.

The separation of the Storting into two divisions was designed for two purposes, impeachment and legislation. Impeachment was established to deal with offenses by people in high government office, i.e., members of the government, members of the Storting, and judges of the Supreme Court. The Odelsting decides whether impeachment shall be applied, while members of the Lagting, together with the Supreme Court, serve as judges of impeachment. During the nineteenth century impeachment was applied at several occasions by the Storting against members of the government, but since the introduction of parliamentarism the institution has passed into disuse.[2]

For legislative purposes the separation into Odelsting and Lagting was introduced in order to ensure that bills could be dealt with by two independent and separate bodies.[3] This procedure pertains to purely legislative matters. It should be added that the right to propose new legislation is limited to the government and to members of the Odelsting. In practice, almost all initiatives come from the government. Decisions concerning taxation are mostly classified as material law and receive separate treatment in the Odelsting and Lagting. But other types of financial matters, above all the budget, are treated by plenary sessions of the Storting.[4]

Another unusual feature of the Norwegian Parliament is its system of deputy members. Regular members of the Storting are represented by deputies (*varamann*) if they are absent from their duties for more than a day or two (Arter, 1984:14 ff.). These deputies are drawn from the unsuccessful candidates on each party's list in the order in which their names appeared on the ballot at the previous election. (For example, if one of the two members of Party X elected in Province Y is absent, then the person listed third on Party X's list becomes a deputy.)

This arrangement has some obvious advantages. While a varamann can rarely be as effective as an experienced member, both the parties and the provinces always have the voting strength they deserve. This minimizes the often unpredictable effects of absences and nonparticipation by individual legislators on collective decisions (see Hall, 1996, on the U.S. Congress). It also involves a significant number of people, over and above the regular membership, in the affairs of the Storting. Service as varamann can be a stepping-stone toward subsequent election to the Storting.

At the beginning of each four-year session, the assembly must also fill its leadership positions. Most important is the choice of presidents (speakers) and leaders of the standing committees. The top officer is the president of the Storting. The assembly also elects a vice president of the Storting, while the Odelsting and the *Lagting* elect their own presidents and vice presidents. This group of six presidents serves as a governing committee for the institution and controls its agenda. Presidents and vice presidents alternate in the chair of their respective assemblies one month at a time. Again, these positions are distributed among the parties proportional to their strength in the Storting. This means, of course, that the Storting leadership includes members who are in opposition to the government of the day.

The Committees

The Storting has a single committee system that serves both of its divisions. Most of the legislature's work is done in private committee meetings, and the plenary sessions of the Storting, Odelsting, and Lagting are devoted to brief debates about, and (usually) ratification of, committee recommendations.

Currently, the Storting has twelve standing committees assigned to policy areas roughly corresponding to those of the government ministries. In addition, the Storting may establish temporary committees to deal with special topics. All members of the Storting, except the president, are required to serve on one, and only one, standing committee. The parties are represented on these committees proportional to their strength in the Storting, and the political parties decide which party members will fill their quota on each committee. The criteria used in making these critically important committee assignments will be analyzed in detail in chapter 9; for now, it is enough to say that the members' preferences and qualifications are considered, along with the party's needs. Reappointments are fairly common; however, members develop no informal right to be reappointed to a committee (as in the American system) and must be assigned de novo every four years. Members whose committee work displeases their fellow partisans risk reassignment to a less desirable committee post in their next term.

The committees have a leader, vice leader, and secretary. These positions are allocated proportionally to the parties and filled by them at the beginning of each four-year term. The governing party (or coalition of governing parties) does not monopolize the committee leadership positions, as majority parties do in the United States. Thus, the formal committee leadership may not be in agreement with government positions.

Each matter arriving at a committee is assigned a spokesperson who presents the committee's recommendations to the Storting as a whole. This responsibility is routinely rotated between the members of the committee without regard to their party. This practice guarantees an active committee membership, weakens the committee leaders, and contributes to consensual policy-making.

The committee system results in a more detailed and informed scrutiny of legislative proposals than would otherwise occur. Committee members become specialists in their policy domains, and their conclusions carry much weight with their colleagues, who are specialists in other areas. The fact that committee meetings are closed to the public[5] facilitates compromise across party lines. The committees thus provide the main arena for power sharing between the parties and between the government and the Storting. Storting committees are unusually powerful for a parliamentary system.

Parliamentary Parties

At the beginning of each electoral period, the members of each party elect a parliamentary leader, a whip, and a secretary. The parliamentary groups meet regularly each week when the Storting is in session. The party group decides what the party's position should be when the party platform is vague or when new issues arrive on the scene. During these debates, the members who serve on committees with jurisdiction for the issues under discussion play especially important roles.[6]

The various parliamentary parties' relationships with their electoral parties differ somewhat. The Labor Party has, from its earliest days, stressed the need for party solidarity and party loyalty from leaders and rank and file alike. This results in a greater formal subordination of the parliamentary group to the electoral organization, mitigated by the fact that the leader of both branches of the party is usually the same person. In the bourgeois parties, the parliamentary group is usually more independent of the electoral organization, although the party manifesto is still expected to bind members.

All the parliamentary parties display high levels of party unity. Bo Bjurulf and Ingemar Glans (1976) found that most parties were cohesive on more than 90 percent of the issues upon which roll calls were held in the early 1970s. William Shaffer (1991) reported an 84 percent figure for the mid-1980s. Hanne Marit Teigum (1995) concluded, perhaps surprisingly, that party cohesiveness was not confined to the core issues of the parties and party unity was high on all types of issues.[7] Dissent on local issues is the easiest for the party leadership to tolerate, and party unity does sometimes break down on issues reflecting strong local interests (Bjurulf and Glans, 1976). Moreover, the issues raised by individual representatives at the "Question Hour"—an opportunity each week for Storting members to ask questions of members of the government (see Arter, 1984: 334 ff., for details)—reflect to a considerable extent local and regional interest articulation rather than partisan concerns (Heidar, 1995b: 9). The importance of local ties is recognized by the party leadership; however, for most purposes the party leaders demand loyalty to the party line, particularly if the issue is addressed in the party program. This principle goes for both voting and debates in the Storting's plenary sessions (Heidar, 1996).

Executive-Legislative Relations

Many contemporary observers of politics in Western democracies have found that parliaments and legislatures have lost significant power to executives in recent decades (King, 1976, for example). The late twentieth century, so the argument goes, has been characterized by an explosive growth in the number, scope, complexity, and inter-relatedness of public problems. Popular expectations about what governments should do about them have escalated, too. Political executives have expertise, and they can make decisions rapidly and in secret, if need be. Large groups of politicians can't. Thus power gravitates toward executives—prime ministers, cabinets, civil servants—by default. Arguments along these lines are common in Norway (Seip, 1963; Hernes, 1971, 1983; Arter, 1984, are a few examples). We recommend a closer look at legislative-executive relations in Norway before accepting this view in its entirety.

Prime ministers are invariably drawn from the Storting; their cabinets are mostly recruited from there as well. In the current government (Jagland I in 1996) about two-thirds (63 percent) of the government served in the Storting at the time of their appointment. But neither prime ministers nor cabinet ministers can continue to serve in the Storting while holding executive position—an element of the separation of powers doctrine that has survived in the Constitution even after the introduction of parliamentarism (Hernes and Nergaard, 1989; Lane and Narud, 1994). If called to the government, Storting members must give up their seat as long as they serve in the government. A deputy representative takes the seat temporarily. Ministers may be asked to appear in the Storting, or in any of its subdivisions, to answer questions and provide information, but they have no vote. The constitutional obligation of the government to keep the Storting informed about current policies is strictly observed (Berggrav, 1994), and failure to do so can have serious consequences

(Hernes and Nergaard, 1989; Rasch, 1994). Prime ministers cannot count on automatic support of government policies in legislative voting, as prime ministers in the U.K. and many other parliamentary countries can.

In order to survive a Norwegian government needs the expressed or silent support of a majority in the Storting. Norway falls into the category of what has been labeled negative parliamentarism (Bergmann, 1993). If a majority of the representatives support a vote of no confidence the government is legally obliged to resign. A majority may also overturn governments as a result of parliamentary questions in which the government threatens to resign if it does not obtain the required support. These procedures do not differ much from one parliamentary system to another. However, the Norwegian system does contain some deviant patterns.

First of all, as we pointed out earlier minority parliamentarism is regarded as acceptable. In fact, since Labor lost its majority position at the beginning of the 1960s it has become more or less the norm for government formation.[8] In multiparty systems in which no single party obtains more than 50 percent of the parliamentary seats, majority-based coalition governments would seem to be a natural solution, and in most multiparty countries this is indeed the case. In this respect Norway, along with Sweden and Denmark, deviates (Strøm, 1984, 1990; Rommetvedt, 1991; Narud, 1996a). For long periods these countries have been run by minority governments, either single-party governments or minority coalitions, that in order to remain in power have been forced to seek additional support in the Parliament from some other party or parties. It is a kind of parliamentarism based on shifting coalitions from one issue to the next. This, in effect, gives the parliamentary opposition considerable influence on the government, since government policy will be a result of compromises and negotiations with opposition parties. Clearly, as pointed out by Strøm (1990) in his excellent work on minority parliamentarism, this expectation is based on the nature of the dominant issues as well as on the organizational characteristics of the Storting. But there can be little doubt that minority rule and parliamentary influence are mutually reinforcing (Strøm, 1990: 207). Moreover, in order to facilitate cooperation in a minority situation, in 1961 the governing party increased the number of opposition members on the board of presidents from two to three. This body of respected parliamentary leaders forms an important setting for communication and compromises between the government and the opposition (Strøm, 1990: 208).

Another deviant aspect of the Norwegian parliamentary system has to do with the right to call for early elections. In Norway the government is not entitled to dissolve the Storting between elections, a prerogative that is applied in nearly all other parliamentary democracies. The possibility of calling a new election provides an important power to the executive. And the fact that Norwegian governments lack this control mechanism clearly enhances the power of the legislative body relative to the executive. Of course, without this recourse to early parliamentary dissolution, the government party or parties are not in a position to schedule elections to their own benefit. And for coalition governments it means that no formal provision for coalition discipline exists in case of conflicts within the cabinet.

A third factor that has been discussed, and that has been taken as an indication of a declining Parliament, is the development of a corporatist structure. Stein Rokkan (1966), for instance, found the corporative/functional channel to be more important than the territorial/election channel. And Robert Kvavik (1976: 120) in his studies of organized interest groups in Norway argued that, instead of using the parliamentary channel of influence, leaders of all the interest organizations preferred the corporate channels. This view was later supported by Gudmund Hernes, who, as a part of the Norwegian Power Studies, concluded: "Power has moved away from the Storting towards the bureaucracy and the interest organization" (1983: 303). Hence, since the Storting has never been closely connected to the corporatist network, this has been taken as an indication of the political impotence of Parliament.

There are several reasons for not accepting such a view. First of all, cabinet members do not have more extensive ties with corporatist institutions than do members of Parliament, yet it is seldom argued that the government is powerless (Strøm, 1990: 207). Second, corporatist interests are already incorporated in the legislative body through interest representation in the process of candidate selection (see chaps. 5 and 8 below). This is true concerning some parties more than others. During Labor nominations the trade unions have an important position when ticket balancing takes place. In addition, they have their own representative present at all Labor Party parliamentary group meetings, and this representative is not considered an external actor but rather a member of the family (Heidar, 1995a: 290). Moreover, frequent contacts exist between representatives for organized interests and members of Parliament. As we shall see in chapter 9, Storting committees are important links for corporatist interests in their attempts to influence government decision-making.

Finally, compared to the Swedish Riksdag and the U.S. Congress, for instance, secretarial assistance and research resources are scarce in the Storting, and what there is is controlled by and large by the party groups, not by the individual representatives (Heidar, 1995b). This increases the power of the party over the individual representatives. The fact that other available resources are mostly located in the civil services gives the government branches considerable influence on parliamentary decision-making. Compared to the individual parliamentarians the civil services have considerable professional experience and skills and are thus in a position to define major premises for political decisions. Moreover, membership turnover in the standing committees has increased substantially since the late 1980s, a tendency that further weakens the professional skills of the legislators.

National legislatures everywhere have experienced difficulties in adapting to their rapidly changing environments in the twentieth century. The Storting is no exception. But we do not believe that the Storting is thus inevitably dominated by the government of the day. We are inclined to agree with Johan P. Olsen's view that "the Storting does not follow a pattern of steady decline from a peak during the 1880s. Rather, the data suggests an ebb-and-flow perspective. . . . Our interpretation is that during the last part of the 1970s, the Storting became a more rather than a less significant institution" (1983: 42, 72).

The Storting and Consensus Democracy

In this chapter we have stressed the things that are unique, or at least unusual, about the Norwegian Storting. We have done this partly because some readers of this book will not know much about Norwegian politics. But also we believe that some of these unusual features of the Storting may help explain the survival of much of its power and independence until the very end of the twentieth century. It is a system with strong, disciplined, programmatic political parties at its core. The parties stress their differences in the ceaseless competition for votes. But the Storting requires cooperation across party lines if the country is to be governed. Consistent with the consensus model, leadership positions such as membership on the board of presidents and chairmanships of the standing committees are distributed among the political parties proportional to their strength. Moreover, the committee system serves as an arena for compromise and cooperation, while the debates on the floor are the place for parties to stress their differences. Whether in opposition or holding power, every party has an opportunity to influence policy decisions. The Storting is where governments share their power with legislators and where political parties share power with each other.

5

Choosing Storting Members

Every four years, two and a half million Norwegians go to the polls to elect their national Parliament. These voters determine the relative strength of the political parties in the Storting; this in turn affects which party or parties will govern and to what ends. The men and women elected to the Storting constitute that institution's supply of talent for the next four years. The prime minister, and most cabinet officers, will be chosen from this same small talent pool. Elections matter.

Yet the Norwegian voters choose from limited alternatives. Political parties—in recent years there have been six major ones—present lists of candidates for the Storting ranked in the order in which the party wishes to see them elected. Voters are permitted to change these lists by crossing out the name of one or more nominated candidates. In practice, such deletions by individual voters have no impact on the final result. Too many voters must make the same change in order to overrule the rankings on the list and the voters have never successfully changed a party's rankings in Storting elections. Thus, Norwegian voters choose from a handful of party lists. The making of these lists—candidate selection—is very important, too.

In this chapter we describe the candidate selection process in contemporary Norway and discuss its consequences for political representation. How well do these processes ensure that the interests of the absent others—ordinary people not directly involved in the nominating process—are represented in policy, service or symbolic ways?

Rules of the Game

The process by which party lists are made is governed by the Norwegian Act of Nominations, which in 1920 established a system resembling the party nominating conventions used in the United States at that time.[1]

This statute is not mandatory, but parties must adhere to its provisions if they wish to obtain public funds to pay for their conventions. Most do. Besides there has been little controversy about nominating procedures in Norway, unlike in the United States, where nominating conventions have been attacked as undemocratic and largely abandoned in favor of direct primary elections.

There are nineteen constituencies in Storting elections—one for each of the eighteen provinces (*fylker*) and one for the city of Oslo. The number of seats per constituency varies from four to fifteen, roughly depending upon population. The parties must develop ranked lists of candidates for each constituency equal to the number of seats assigned to their constituency plus up to six additional candidates. Thus parties in small constituencies with only four seats in the Storting will normally develop lists of ten ranked candidates. In Oslo, the largest electoral district with fifteen seats, the party lists usually consist of twenty-one names. Only candidates toward the top of these lists have any chance of election, although a larger number will serve briefly as alternates or varamann.

The electoral lists are constructed by party conventions held in each constituency consisting of 20 to 150 delegates. These delegates are elected at local meetings in which all dues-paying party members of voting age may participate, the number of delegates from each locality depending upon the number of votes garnered by the party at the last Storting election. Before these meetings, the provincial party officers appoint a small (five- to fifteen-member) nominating committee that, after consultation and input from the local party meetings, proposes a list of candidates to the convention. This proposed list of candidates structures debate at the convention, but the candidate for each position on the list must be adopted by majority vote, which is by no means assured. The decisions of the provincial conventions, according to the Act of Nominations, are final and cannot be overruled by public authority or by the national party. (The law does permit the provincial conventions to submit their list to a referendum among party members, but no such referendum has been held to date.)

The "Selectorate"

The candidate selection process in Norway is an internal political party affair. Only dues-paying party members can participate in candidate selection meetings. While these dues are low, party members are a small fraction—about 15 percent—of all voters (table 5.1). And only about

Table 5.1

The Selectorate, by Party, 1985

Party	Party Members: % of voters[a]	Participated in Nomination Process: % of voters[a]	Number of Delegates in Nominating Conventions[b]	Delegates as % of Voters	Delegates as % of Members
Socialist Left	11	9	1,433	1.1	9.2
Labor	15	4	2,806	0.3	1.8
Liberal	21	7	710	0.7	4.2
Christian People's	29	8	1,260	0.6	2.0
Center	26	5	988	0.6	2.2
Conservative	16	3	2,787	0.4	2.2
Progress	8	8	703	0.6	9.2
All parties	15	5	10,687	0.6	4.5

[a]Figures from 1985 election survey.

[b]Estimated on the basis of 1981 election statistics. Figures for Oslo were obtained directly from the parties.

Table 5.2
Political Activity and Interest in Politics (%)

Level of Political Interest	Level of Activity			
	Non-Voter	Voter	Party Member	Attended Local or Provincial Party Meetings
Very interested	3	8	22	31
Somewhat interested	24	32	43	49
Total interested	27	40	65	80
Little interest	55	53	33	17
No interest	18	7	2	3
Total	100	100	100	100
N	262	1,840	328	99

one-third of all party members—about 5 percent of all voters—report having participated in the nominating process. Our best estimate of the number of delegates attending provincial nominating conventions in 1985 is under 11,000, considerably less than 1 percent of those who voted in the national election that year.[2]

Entrusting the making of party electoral lists to such a small circle is not without risk of oligarchy—control over nominations by a self-perpetuating and self-serving elite. Indeed, it has been argued that oligarchy is an inescapable property of political parties (Michels, 1949). But let us not assume "the iron law of oligarchy." Rather, we shall examine the characteristics of those who are actively engaged in making party nominations—the "selectorate"—and how they behave before coming to such a gloomy conclusion.

The Norwegian selectorate differs from the Norwegian electorate in very significant ways. First, its members are much more interested in politics. Eighty percent of those taking part in nominating committee meetings in 1985 were "very" or "somewhat" interested in politics (table 5.2). Those who took part in the meetings without being interested were presumably dragged along by someone who was—a politically involved spouse, friend, or co-worker. The ordinary Norwegian finds politics uninteresting. This is true in other democratic societies, of course. But in Norway voting is an obligation that even the disinterested usually honor—59 percent of those who said they had no interest in politics also report that they voted in 1958. This obligation does not, however, extend to more demanding forms of political participation such as paying dues or going to meetings. Perhaps the most important attribute of the Norwegian selectorate is that it is voluntary, a largely self-selected group of interested people.

A second characteristic of the Norwegian selectorate is that it consists heavily of experienced elective officials, both public and party. Our data here are drawn from our survey of the members of party nominating committees, the small group appointed by the provincial party organizations to put together the initial list of names presented to the provincial conventions. On the average 42 percent of those groups were currently members of city councils in 1985 and 13 percent belonged to provincial councils (table 5.3). Members of other city and provincial boards and committees were also very common, although most of these memberships were held by members of the city and provincial councils.

Much the same picture is found when our attention is shifted to political party activity and achievement. Most of the members of the nominating committees have been active party people for many years, primarily at the city or provincial levels. Ninety percent of the members of the 1985 nominating committees had taken an active part in at least one previous Storting nomination process, and the average member had taken part in several. More than a quarter of the nominating committee members had served on one or more nominating committees in earlier years. All of these generalizations hold true for all the parties. Thus the Storting's selectorate consists of highly motivated party activists, many with experience in elected local or provincial office, who tend to be actively involved in Storting nominations over several national elections.

A third characteristic of the selectorate is that it differs in social and economic background from the average Norwegian. Here again, our data are from our survey of nominating committee members (table 5.4). Those critically significant actors tend to be, at least in 1985, middle-aged to elderly males with university educations and high-status occupations. There are some differences here between the parties, but they are either small or expected—i.e., more workers in the Labor Party, more businessmen in Høyre, more farmers in the Center Party. High social status tends to be associated with high levels of political activity everywhere (Matthews, 1954; Putnam, 1976). Norway is no exception.

The fact remains that the nominating committees are not very representative of Norway in the backgrounds and experience of their members.

Table 5.3

Political Backgrounds of Nominating Committee Members, 1985

Local Government Position	%	Years of Party Activity	%	Party Position	%	Previous Nominating Conventions Attended	%
City council	42	1–5	19	Local board	48	0	10
Provincial council	13	6–10	32	Provincial board	29	1	28
City government committees	52	11–15	19	Women's org.	7	2	25
Other provincial committees	21	16–20	14	Youth org.	7	3	18
Other community committees	5	21–25	7	Central Party	3	4	11
DK	2	26+	7	Unspecified activity	8	5+	8
		DK	2				

Note: DK = don't know.

Table 5.4

Social and Economic Backgrounds of Nominating
Committee Members, 1985

	Nominating Committee Members (%)	All Norwegians of Voting Age[a] (%)
Age		
Under 30	13	25
31–50	55	51
Over 50	32	24
Total	100	100
Sex		
Male	63	52
Female	37	48
Total	100	100
Education[a]		
Primary and secondary	8	29
Gymnas or occupational schooling	42	55
University	50	16
Total	100	98 (2% DK)
Occupation		
Professional	2	3
High functionary	36	8
Self-employed in trade, industry, or commerce	6	3
Low functionary	11	25
Farmers and fishermen	7	4
Workers	10	24
Housewives	8	9
Students	5	4
Retired persons	2	16
Others, not ascertained	13	6
Total	100	100

Note: DK = don't know.

[a]Highest level attended.

Decentralization

The concept of a selectorate is useful because it focuses attention on the attributes of the people actively engaged in nominating politics. But these people behave in patterned or structured ways. The most important structural feature of Norwegian party nominations is decentralization: nominations are dominated by local and provincial elites.

The Act of Nominations does not permit national party leaders to interfere directly in nomination proceedings in individual constituencies, and they have no veto over the decisions of the conventions. The constituencies of Oslo and Akershus (the province surrounding Oslo), are exceptions. Since the parties have their national headquarters in the capital, the top leaders tend to be involved in the party branches of those provinces, and many of them are nominated for election there. Party branches in other constituencies, however, seem to be zealous defenders of their autonomy.

An illuminating incident occurred at the 1985 Labor Party nominations. The previous year the party's national convention introduced a gender quota for nominations in order to improve the representation of women in Parliament.[3] At the 1985 election this rule was generally accepted by the party branches, except in the constituency of Sogn og Fjordane on the west coast. In this constituency, in which Labor could hope to obtain two seats at most, the two top candidates from the preceding election, both men, were renominated and ranked first and second. This led to an outcry in the Labor women's movement, which appealed to the national leaders to support its demand that one candidate should be replaced by a woman. Both the executive committee and the national committee recommended that the party in Sogn og Fjordane reconsider the nomination. But the constituency party refused to obey, referring to the rule in the Act of Nominations saying that decisions of a nominating convention are final. The central leaders had no choice but to accept the situation. A direct confrontation between national and constituency leaders was unthinkable, partly because it implied violation of the electoral law, partly because politically it might ruin the party's electoral chances in the constituency. At a few recent elections the Labor Party had suffered from internal splits over issues related to territorial divisions in Sogn og Fjordane. The balancing of these district interests was a major concern when the constituency convention composed its 1985 electoral list.

National party leaders who might wish to influence nominations are politically unable to do so through direct interference, except perhaps in

Oslo and Akershus. The question remains, however, whether they can do so indirectly. For one thing, leaders can appoint prospective candidates to positions of high prestige and visibility. This method is particularly applicable to parties holding power. By appointing somebody as a member of the government, or as chair of some important committee, they can bring him to public attention and thus strengthen his chances for nomination—provided he is otherwise acceptable to his home constituency.[4]

Furthermore, national leaders can conceivably influence the constituency level by working through informal networks inside their respective parties. As indicated above, the nomination committee holds a key position in the proceedings of the convention. This committee would therefore be the best arena for leaders to influence decisions, although (officially at least) national party headquarters are not informed about the composition of nomination committees in the various constituencies. How do national leaders fit into the internal channels of communication as reported by members of nomination committees?

Our study of the 1985 nomination committees confirms that there is little contact between national party leaders and committee members. The respondents were asked: "Which of the following groups contacted you about the selection of candidates?" (The names of the groups are indicated in table 5.5.) Only one of ten respondents reported that they had been contacted by national leaders. A somewhat higher proportion indicated contact with members of the Storting. Nearly three out of ten were contacted by potential candidates. The main message conveyed by table 5.5 is that most of the discussion was with local politicians as well as leaders of local party organizations. The discussions that did occur with national leaders and Storting members were, more often than not, initiated by the nominating committee member. Finally, 20 percent of the respondents reported having been contacted by leaders of organizations outside the parties. This figure is not surprising, considering the strong corporatist tendencies in modern Norwegian society.

Some striking differences between parties emerge from the table. Without entering into a detailed analysis, a few tendencies deserve mention. Although contacts with local and provincial leaders appear to be equally important in all parties, local politicians were mentioned least frequently in the Socialist Left and the Progress parties. The explanation is that these small parties have relatively few representatives in local office. A similar explanation may probably be applied when small parties report relatively low contact with members of the Storting. The possibility of contact is limited by the small number of party representatives. However, the

Table 5.5

Contacts with Nominating Committees (%)

Party	Aspirants		Members of Storting		National Party Leaders		Mayors, Local Office-holders		Provincial/ Local Party Leaders		Groups Outside the Party		N
	Other Initiated	R Initiated	Other	R	Other	R	Other	R	Other	R	Other	R	
Socialist Left	17	53	4	9	15	18	16	17	83	83	17	13	76
Labor	28	34	22	35	1	6	53	46	84	79	33	21	109
Liberal	15	48	2	8	15	17	35	33	83	87	19	10	52
Christian People's	17	42	16	24	10	11	34	48	77	80	18	12	95
Center	10	34	7	13	4	7	41	50	74	89	10	10	68
Conservative	43	63	38	55	10	12	55	50	90	89	22	15	103
Progress	64	67	11	22	20	27	24	18	93	87	9	7	45
All parties	27	47	17	27	9	13	39	40	83	83	20	14	548

Note: R = nominating committee members.

relatively large number of Conservatives mentioning this kind of contact suggests that it is not only the size of representation that counts. After all, the Labor Party has a larger parliamentary group than the Conservatives. According to long tradition, the parliamentary group constitutes the most important center of power in the Conservative Party (Sejersted, 1984: 198–200). The fact that Conservative respondents were most inclined to mention contacts with parliamentarians may well reflect the power structure of the party. In the Labor Party, by comparison, the party organization outside Parliament tends to wield relatively more power.

Respondents of three parties—Socialist Left, Liberal, and Progress—were more inclined to mention contact with national party leaders. This may simply mean that parties with only a handful of representatives in Parliament feel more need than larger parties to choose candidates who can perform certain roles in parliamentary work.

It is not surprising that few respondents report having been contacted by aspirants. In Norwegian political culture it is not considered good manners to advocate one's own political career, with a notable exception for persons who have already been representatives to the Storting. Table 5.5 indicates a striking difference between the two parties to the right—Conservatives and Progress—and all other parties, with respondents of the former parties reporting greater contact by aspirants. Aggressive self-promotion is consistent with the liberalistic values prevalent in the parties to the right (Valen and Aardal, 1983: 146). Finally, contacts with groups outside the parties were most frequently mentioned by Labor respondents. This probably reflects the close ties between Labor and the trade union movement. Outside contacts were reported also in other parties, in particular the Conservative Party, which has close links to business.

In summary, the data support the notion of a highly decentralized nomination process conducted by local party activists in the country's nineteen semi-autonomous constituencies. National leaders may try to influence these proceedings, but they do not control them. "Every election year we send out a letter suggesting that they choose some candidates who are not farmers," a national leader of the Center Party told one of the authors with a shrug. "Every year our lists continue to be mostly farmers."

Slate-Making

Norwegian party conventions all confront the same task—to decide upon a strong list of candidates. But what that means, practically speaking, can differ depending on the constituency, the party and perhaps other

Table 5.6
Members of Storting by Ballot Position, 1985

Ballot Position	Party						Total	%
	DNA	H	KrF	Sp	SV	FrP		
1st	19	19	12	11	6	2	69	44
2nd	19	13	4	1	0	0	37	24
3rd	16	9	0	0	0	0	25	16
4th	10	4	0	0	0	0	14	9
5th	6	3	0	0	0	0	9	6
6th	1	1	0	0	0	0	2	1
7th	0	1	0	0	0	0	1	1
Total	71	50	16	12	6	2	157	100

factors. The number of names on the lists, for example, varies from about ten to about twenty; the number of these with any chance of election ranges from none to a handful. More than a few conventions confront the problem of recruiting an entire slate facing certain defeat, while most conventions can expect considerable competition at least for the few positions on the list that may lead to the Storting. The size of this top group varies: small parties rarely elect more than one member per constituency (table 5.6). This candidate needs to be acceptable, or at least more acceptable than anyone else, to the various factions and perspectives within the party. Where the convention expects to fill four, five, or six seats, the top candidates can, perhaps, be harder edged, with more specialized appeals, so long as the entire top group is appropriately balanced.

These conjectures are only partially supported by our survey of nominating committee members. When asked to name the personal qualities a top candidate should possess, the committee members showed surprising agreement. Top candidates, first and foremost, need to enjoy the trust and confidence of their party, be good campaigners (with eloquence, charisma, media skills, and so on), and be politically experienced (table 5.7). Other factors were mentioned—activity within the party, support from outside groups, gender, age, and so on—but did not figure largely in their answers. Differences in these responses by members of different parties and from different types of constituencies were small and seemingly random. Much the same set of personal attributes ranked highest for those candidates with little chance of election. However, party maintenance and ticket-balancing considerations were assigned greater import than at the top of the ballot—a candidate's age and sex, relationships with important groups and associations, and record of service to the party

Table 5.7

Qualities Desired in Candidates, 1985

(In % of All Attributes Mentioned)

Quality of Candidate	Top Candidates	Other Candidates
Enjoys confidence of party	25	20
Ability at campaigning	24	16
Experience in public office	22	9
Active in party organization	10	15
Independent in relations with groups	7	4
Gender	3	6
Has support in important organizations	6	10
Represents youth	1	9
Associated with specific occupational groups	1	4
N	1,658	1,614

Note: Respondents were asked to give three attributes for top candidates (undefined) and another three attributes for other candidates.

were believed to be more important than for the top people on the list. In general, the data suggest that abilities as a professional politician are strongly required for top candidates, while the less important places on the list can be used to make a symbolic appeal to groups of voters and to reward faithful workers in the party organization.

Other preferences of the nominating conventions can be inferred by the character of the electoral lists themselves. Between 30 and 40 percent of the names on the electoral lists were on the lists four years before. Most nominating committees, it seems, begin their task by canvassing all those nominated at the last Storting election to see if they wish to be renominated. Obviously, many say "yes." The tendency to nominate people more than once used to be more pronounced in the Labor and Communist parties than in the bourgeois parties, but since the 1960s the pattern seems to have disappeared and all the parties now renominate between 30 and 40 percent of their candidates. Once elected to the Storting renomination is likely—most who are not renominated have voluntarily withdrawn from consideration (some, no doubt, because of uncertainty about what would happen if they remained in the race). Storting members and nominees from earlier elections are very prominent in the electoral lists of all parties—not surprising, given the selectorate's strong preference for political experience.

The importance of geography in slate-making is also evident from even a casual look at the parties' electoral lists. Except for some of the largest cities, two candidates ranked next to each other rarely come from the same commune or even from neighboring communes (the candidates' place of residence and occupation are listed on the ballot below their names). Norwegian electoral districts are large, and various parts of these provinces can have different interests when it comes to the construction of roads, the location of schools and hospitals, the development of new industries, and the like. Parties in the Oslo electoral district, consisting of a single commune, do not pay as much attention to the geographical location of their candidates.

In recent years, the gender of candidates has taken on great importance. Traditionally, the parties nominated only a few women in each constituency, mostly among the lower candidates. Recent years, however, have witnessed growing demands for representation equal to that of men. The election of 1985 constituted a major breakthrough. A quota system introduced by the parties of the left assured a high proportion of women not only among the total number of candidates nominated, but also among the top candidates (Valen, 1986). These parties tended to nominate men and women alternately from top to bottom of the list. But, as demonstrated in the Sogn og Fjordane case, even a quota system does not guarantee equality of representation.

Why is ticket-balancing important? For one thing, through ticket-balancing parties are able to appeal directly to the voters. Arguments for or against specific candidates almost invariably refer to the expectations and likely reactions of the electorate. Hence it may be argued that considerations of voters' preferences serve as the ultimate legitimacy in the selection of candidates. But do voters really know candidates? In a nationwide representative voter survey of the 1985 election the respondents were asked to identify candidates in their constituency by name. The data revealed a low level of knowledge: a third of respondents were unable to name a single candidate, while only 39 percent could identify three or more. As might be expected, there was a substantial difference between party members and ordinary voters. In the latter group 37 percent were unable to name correctly a single candidate, while the corresponding figure for members was 16 percent. Despite lack of information about the candidates, ticket-balancing implies that a variety of voters' demands have to be recognized. Voters may not know the names of candidates, but still can often recognize them on a list and have a generally favorable or unfavorable impression of the kinds of people found on the various parties' lists.

Second, ticket-balancing constitutes a link between parties and organizations in the community. One of the major functions of political parties is to aggregate a variety of social interests (Almond and Coleman, 1960). This can be furthered through selection of candidates. By nominating candidates who belong to several different organizations, parties present an image of concern about a variety of social interests without being narrowly committed to a specific group or policy program.

Third, ticket-balancing fulfills important functions inside the party. It provides the convention with a mechanism for choosing among a number of eligible aspirants and serves to reduce intra-party conflicts in the selection process. At the same time ticket-balancing implies competition between internal subgroups. By being represented on the list groups are given visible access to party leadership and are thus encouraged to render the party their active and loyal support.

Nominations and Representation

Who is nominated to run in Storting elections matters. Members of the Parliament are expected to follow their respective party's line and rarely vote independently. But electoral mandates on the specific issues coming before the Storting are frequently vague, overly general, outdated by events, or entirely absent (see chap. 7). The party line is thus often what the Storting party delegations collectively decide it is. The Storting is a major training and recruiting grounds for prime ministers and cabinet officials. The human makeup of the Storting is symbolically significant, contributing to or detracting from the legitimacy of its decisions. But are the interests of the absent others adequately represented in Norwegian nominations?

The small number of Norwegians who take a direct part in nominating politics is not comforting on this score. Nor is the fact that the Norwegian selectorate has consisted mainly of middle-aged, upper-middle-class men. In a comparative perspective, however, this trend is not particularly surprising, since the same two tendencies exist in most other countries (Gallagher and Marsh, 1988: 245–47; Putnam, 1976). A distinguishing feature in the Norwegian selectorate is that a large number of members are experienced elective politicians, both within their parties and in local government. The criteria they employ in making nominating decisions place much weight on popularity with voters and vote-getting potential.

Moreover, the Norwegian nominating system is open and competitive in several ways. Entry to the decision process is easy: pay a party's dues and attend a local meeting and you have joined a party's selectorate. A few people who are unhappy about their party's list can have a big impact at poorly attended local meetings. Most of the time Norwegian voters are content to leave all this to "the politicians." But if the politicians make decisions that enrage even a small fraction of their fellow partisans, they can be overwhelmed in the next round of local party meetings packed with the formerly quiescent. The way for party selectorates to protect their own influence is to try to keep everybody in the party happy, to please, or at least not displease, the absent others. This, of course, is made easier by the inattention that usually characterizes nominating politics in Norway (and just about everywhere else). It should be noted, however, that media attention to nominations has increased substantially during the last couple of decades (Narud, 1994).

Members of the selectorate not only want to protect their own interests, they also want their party to win. A popular list of candidates contributes to that end, or so they believe. While the competition for seats in the Storting is zero sum—that is, the only way that a party can increase its seats in the Storting is by taking them away from another party—electoral competition in Norway does not have the dog-eat-dog ferocity usually found in zero-sum situations. No party, in recent decades, can reasonably expect to win a majority of the seats in the Storting; some kind of cooperation between parties is required to govern, either as coalition or minority government, once the election is over. Most of the smaller parties are more interested in guarding their base support in the electorate and niche in the legislature than in drastically expanding their following. All of this takes some of the sharp edges off electoral competition.

But competition there is. Political parties succeed or fail, come and go, depending upon their success in attracting voters. Two major parties— the Communist and Venstre—recently have disappeared from the halls of the Storting because their program and candidates were no longer popular. Three of today's parties—Socialist Left, Christian People's, and Progress—have become major parties since World War II.

In free-market systems, according to classical economic theory, competition ensures consumer sovereignty. The competitive nominating system in Norway departs too far from this model—too few parties, too high exit and entry costs, too ill-informed consumers, and so on—to guarantee voter sovereignty. The better economic analogy is that of oligopoly, a system characterized by somewhat muted competition between a limited number of units. While the results may fall short of an ideal outcome, they come a great deal closer to the ideal than the absence of competition altogether.

6

Voters and the Storting

S tudies of representation have usually focused on representatives and their attitudes, behavior, and expectations. Less is known about the role of the electors in the process of representation. Twenty years ago, John Wahlke (1978) called for more inquiry into public orientations towards representative institutions. He was concerned especially with "the incidence and variations of support" in different systems. Some interesting research along these lines has appeared (see Jewell, 1985), but the role of the represented remains understudied. Yet in most thinking about representative democracy, it is the voters who drive the process.

In this book we focus primarily on the relationship between voters and members of the Storting and on the institutions that shape that relationship. In this chapter, we concentrate on the voters alone. We shall look at how voters evaluate the Storting and how this compares with popular evaluations of legislatures in other countries. We then will examine how much and in what ways Norwegians participate in Storting elections and decision-making in between elections. We shall demonstrate the importance of political parties and voluntary private associations as channels of communication between rulers and the ruled. We suggest four patterns of citizen participation and speculate about the contributions, both positive and negative, these types make to representative government in Norway. Finally, we shall study the political opinions of Norwegian voters and how these opinions are organized.

Evaluations of the Storting

How the public evaluates its political institutions is crucial. A "reservoir of good will" or "diffuse support" seems essential to long-term institutional effectiveness (Easton, 1966). Public support may be seen as an index of the legitimacy of public policy decisions. Little trust in politicians and

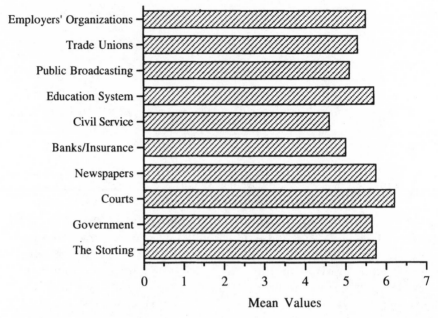

Figure 6.1 Confidence in Norwegian Institutions, 1989. *Source:* Norwegian general election survey of 1989.

elected bodies reflects a low level of felt-responsiveness to citizens' wants and needs (Patterson et al. 1991: 316).

The Storting is highly regarded in comparison both with other Norwegian institutions and with legislatures in other countries. This conclusion is based upon data gathered by others, at somewhat different times, using somewhat different questions. Even so, these generalizations are clearly supported by the data.

In figure 6.1, the confidence Norwegians have in various institutions is rated. This data is drawn from the Norwegian general election survey of 1989. Respondents were asked to evaluate various institutions along a 10-point scale, ranging from 1 (very dissatisfied) to 10 (very satisfied). The results show only minor variations from one institution to the next—all are high. The Storting ranked second best after the courts.

Figure 6.2 presents a comparison of public confidence in the Storting and trust of parliaments in other European countries. These data are for 1990 from Ola Listhaug and Matti Wiberg (1992). In this study Norway ranks highest among the fourteen nations studied. Four more countries are above average—Iceland, the Netherlands, Germany, and Ireland. Italy and Portugal are at the bottom.

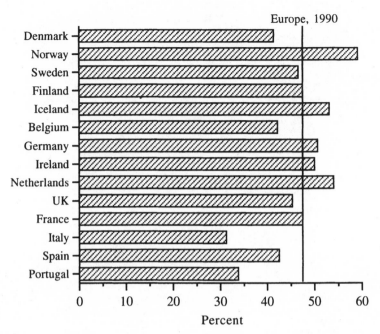

Figure 6.2 Confidence in European Parliaments, 1990. *Source:* Listhaug and Wiberg (1992), 304–5, table 10.1.

Other studies report that public confidence in all political institutions in numerous countries, including Norway, has been declining (Miller, 1974; Rusk and Borre, 1976; Holmberg and Giljam, 1987; Listhaug, 1989; Miller and Listhaug, 1990). Economic hard times, new and seemingly intractable problems, and the spread of liberalistic, antigovernment ideas may have taken their toll on popular confidence in government's ability to solve problems. Confidence and trust, which take years to develop, can erode quickly. Confidence in the Storting has declined in the face of these discontents, but still remains high relative to other Norwegian institutions and to legislatures in other countries.

Voting in Storting Elections

The most important linkages between members of the Storting and the absent others are parliamentary elections, held every four years in Norway.[1] Elections, and the anticipation of them, are thought to give voters

Table 6.1

Average Voter Turnouts (%)

Country	Turnout
Italy[a]	93
Austria[a]	88
Belgium	88
Sweden	86
Australia[a]	86
Denmark	85
West Germany	85
New Zealand	83
Finland	82
NORWAY	82
Netherlands	82
Israel	82
France	78
Spain	78
Ireland	77
United Kingdom	75
Japan	72
Canada	68
United States[b]	54
Switzerland	44

Source: Powell (1986), appendix 1.

[a]Compulsory voting.

[b]Presidential elections.

control over who goes to the Storting and what they do when they get there. Who votes (and who doesn't vote) in Norway?

In recent elections, about 82 percent of all Norwegians who met the legal qualifications for voting have actually voted. This is below the handful of states with compulsory voting but well above the United Kingdom and the U.S. (see table 6.1). The Norwegian voter turnout is about average when compared with other small industrialized democracies in western Europe.

This level of voting was not achieved overnight. In the 1880s and '90s the voter turnout in Norway was comparable to today's rate—about 80 percent—but of course the electorate was very small (see figure 6.3). As the vote was extended to new groups of people—workers, women, young people—turnout sagged by 20 to 30 percentage points, largely the result

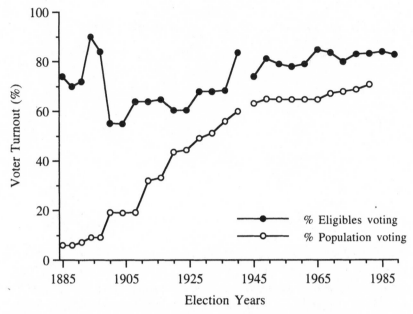

Figure 6.3 Voter Turnout in Storting Elections since 1885. *Sources:* Heidar (1983), 128, table 4.2; Torp (1990), 189.

of low turnout rates of the newly enfranchised. Those who are granted the vote do not immediately or automatically flock to the polls. They need to learn when, where, and how to vote. The parties and politicians must learn how best to appeal to them. In a word, the newly enfranchised must be mobilized. By World War II, the turnout rate in Norway was back in the low 80s but now it was 80 percent of a mass electorate.

Historically the political parties have played an important role in bringing Norwegian voters to the polls. They are in the business of attracting votes. But what role do they play today in an era of television, mass electorates, charismatic candidates, and American-style politics? Table 6.2 suggests that the Norwegian parties remain an important influence on voter turnout.

The relationship between the extent of an individual's identification with any of the Norwegian parties and that individual's voting rate is high. Ninety-four percent of the strong identifiers voted, while only 72 percent of those without partisan ties and 51 percent of those who profess to be apolitical voted. This is a healthy statistical relationship but it is not exactly an iron law. About one-third of those who voted in 1985 had no attachment—be it emotional or cognitive—to a political party.

Table 6.2

Party Identification and Voter Turnout, 1985 (%)

Strength of Party ID	Voted	Did Not Vote
Strong identifiers	94	6
Weak identifiers	86	14
Nonpartisans	72	28
Apoliticals	51	49

gamma = .57 ($p < .0000$).

Let us examine alternative explanations. Many research studies have shown that social and economic status affects voter turnout (see Verba and Nie, 1978: chap. 8 for a short summary). This pattern holds in Norway, too. In table 6.3 we show the rate of participation of several social and economic categories. Gender, for example, seems to make no difference in the rate of voting, but women are a little less likely than men to become party identifiers or dues-paying members of a party. There are fairly large differences in all three types of participation between age groups. Norwegians seem to become more politically active as they grow older.[2] Better-educated people participate more than others when it comes to voting and joining parties. Intriguingly this pattern is reversed when we look at party identification: the less well educated were more likely to develop party identification than those with *gymnas* or university training. Apparently the highly educated in Norway learn that voting is a responsibility, but some also learn to value independence over partisanship.

Could it be that the larger differences in voting rates we originally found between people with differing degrees of partisan identification are really the results of these social and economic differences? In order to answer this question, we must examine both socioeconomic status and strength of party identification simultaneously. In table 6.4, we look at the relationship between gender, age, education level, occupation and voting in 1985, within groups of those who have strong party ID, some party ID, and no party ID. Gender makes no difference in voting turnout, while the strength of party ID among men and women does matter. Ninety-three percent of the men with strong ID voted in 1985; only 70 percent of the men with no party ID voted that year. Looking now at age groupings, we see a similar picture. Differences in age make little difference among those with party identification, but those with no party ID do seem to vote more often (or less often) depending upon their age. The same pattern

Table 6.3
Political Participation in 1985, by SES

	% Voting	% Party Identifiers	% Party Members
Gender			
Male	84	70	18
Female	84	65	12
Age			
30 and younger	77	61	8
31–50	87	63	16
51 and older	86	76	20
Education level			
Elementary	82	74	14
Gymnas I	84	66	13
Gymnas II	84	65	17
University	90	61	17
Occupation level			
Workers	83	71	12
Functionaries	88	64	16
Self-employed	88	68	16
Farmers, fishermen,			
forestry workers	85	75	13
Students	70	53	10

is even clearer for education. How much education one has does not appear to be related to voting rates for party identifiers—they all vote at high frequencies. Among those without a party ID, education matters—only 60 percent of those with grammar school educations voted, while 83 percent of those with university educations voted in 1985. The relationship between occupation and voter turnout also holds up after controlling for level of party ID. Party ID overwhelms SES variables in accounting for voter turnout. SES variables are important for those without party ID.

There is yet another way in which the strong relationship between party ID and voting turnout might be misleading or spurious. Both political interest and political information are positively associated with voting

Table 6.4

Voter Turnout in 1985, by SES and Strength of Party ID (%)

SES	Strength of Party ID			Difference
	Strong Identifiers	Weak Identifiers	No Identifiers	
Gender				
Male	93	85	70	+23
Female	95	87	70	+25
Difference	−2	−2	0	
Age				
30 and younger	91	80	62	+29
31–50	95	90	78	+17
51 and older	95	86	68	+27
Difference	−4	−6	−6	
Education level				
Grammar school	92	85	60	+32
Gymnas 1	93	86	72	+21
Gymnas 2	96	71	71	+25
University	97	90	83	+14
Difference	−5	−5	−23	
Occupation				
Workers	94	84	67	+27
Functionaries	95	91	79	+16
Self-employed	93	96	76	+17
Farmers, fishermen, forestry workers	100	84	57	+43
Students	82	75	59	+23
Difference	−18	−22	−22	

and with having party ID. Perhaps it is these two variables, rather than party ID, that predicts voting rates. After examining table 6.5, that suspicion can be put to rest: party ID has a large impact on voter turnout within groups with the same level of political interest and information. Political interest and political information have large impacts on voter turnout rates of those with no party ID and little, if any, on voter turnout among party identifiers.

Table 6.5
Voter Turnout in 1985, by Political Interest and Knowledge (%)

	Strong Party ID	Weak Party ID	No Party ID	Difference
Political interest				
Very	96	81	83	+13
Somewhat	94	87	81	+13
Little	94	87	71	+23
None	87	76	41	+46
Difference	+9	+11	+42	
Political information				
High	96	96	81	+15
Medium	96	94	79	+17
Low	94	92	77	+17
None	92	81	56	+36
Difference	+4	+15	+25	

Note: Political interest was measured by answers to this question: "Generally, are you very interested in politics, somewhat interested, little interested, or not interested at all?" Political information was measured by the number of candidates running in his/her province that the respondent could name. Five or more names was counted as high, three or four medium, one or two low, and no names identified was zero.

Participation beyond Voting

Voting is not the only way people can and do participate in the political process. They can write or talk to their representatives, try to activate the groups they belong to to take action, write letters, complain, and so on. Especially in recent decades, unconventional direct action—demonstrations, protest marches, sit-ins, and so on—have become popular among those who may have lost patience with the delays and compromises of parliamentary democracy. Symbolic actions staged before the ever hungry eyes of television have become commonplace. Norway has not escaped this trend—in the Alta valley, on the front lawn of the Storting, and elsewhere. And then, of course, the more conventional modes of communications between the ruled and their rulers continue.

To explore this part of the process of representation, we asked the 1985 sample whether they had, during the last four years,

signed petitions in order to promote some specific matter,
participated in demonstrations in order to promote some cause,
written to newspapers to promote some cause,
taken up a cause in party, trade union, or organizations,
made a written complaint, promoted other proposals, and so on,
made contact with some elected representative.

The percentage of all respondents answering "yes" to these queries is as follows (we have reordered the items by their frequency):

19 percent signed petitions,
9 percent approached elected officials,
9 percent took up a cause in party, trade union, or associations,
9 percent took part in demonstrations,
5 percent made complaints,
3 percent wrote to newspapers.

Well over half of those reporting any of these activities engaged in only one of them; only 3 percent engaged in four or more. The most popular of these actions—signing petitions—involves no initiative and little time or energy. All the other figures are low. Most Norwegians vote—even those who profess no interest in politics—but most do little else in the political realm.

Are these activities a substitute for voting? The answer is no. More than 90 percent of those reporting one or more of the activities voted in 1985. These activities are not alternatives to voting, but additional forms of participation.

Participation in Organizations

Private, nonparty organizations and associations play a large role in the process of government in Norway—this point is repeated over and over in the literature and in this book. Does the average Norwegian take an active part in these organizations? And how does activity in this corporatist realm relate to the explicitly political activity we have described above?

In an attempt to explore these questions we asked our respondents: "Are you a member of some trade union, organization for employees, or some other occupational association?" (If "yes"): "Are you an active member of this organization?" Forty-three percent of the respondents men-

Organizations

Parties	Active Members	Others	
Dues-paying members	**Generalist elite** 5%	**Party elite** 10%	15%
Non-members	**Corporative elite** 12%	**Rank and file** 73%	85%
	17%	83%	100%

N = 2,169

Figure 6.4   Membership in Parties and Organizations

tioned belonging to some economic or professional association, and nearly half of these members (18 percent of the total sample) indicated they were active in them. This is a higher level of participation than we found in the political parties. And this participation rate certainly would have been higher if we had not limited our question to occupational organizations alone. Formal membership in these associations is widespread, and a significant minority of Norwegians are actively involved in them.

Three Types of Activists

Both parties and organizations are causes and effects of citizen participation. Let us look at the interaction between these two channels of communication. Figure 6.4 shows the basic situation. Voters who are party members and at the same time active members of some organization are called the generalist elite. They constitute 5 percent of the sample. On the other extreme are the rank and file, nonmembers of parties and nonmembers or inactive members of organizations. Three out of four voters belong to this category. The two other categories are especially interesting from our point of view: the party elite, i.e., members of parties, but without active positions in organizations (10 percent of the sample) and

Table 6.6

Political Activity and Elite Position: % Reporting Activity

	Voted in 1985	Signed Petitions	Participated in Demonstrations, Actions	Wrote Complaints	Wrote to Newspapers	Promoted Cause in Party/Org.	Contacted Representatives
Generalist elite	96	39	22	26	14	45	47
Corporate elite	88	25	10	10	10	17	20
Party elite	99	29	19	6	4	23	15
Rank-and file	86	15	6	2	2	3	4

the corporative elite, i.e., activists in organizations, but not party members (12 percent). The political activity of these four types of Norwegians is presented in table 6.6.

As might be expected the generalist elite is most active on almost all items. Notice in particular that nearly half of these respondents have indicated attempts to promote some cause in party and/or organizations or have been in direct contact with elected representatives. For rank-and-file voters, on the other hand, political activity beyond the act of voting is negligible, except for the signing of petitions. Party elites and corporatist elites fall in the middle. Differences between these two groups are small. However, the party elite is more likely to vote than the corporatist group and more likely to have promoted causes.

The groups included in table 6.6 differ enormously regarding political participation. Most striking is the difference between the rank and file and the three elite groups. Who are attracted to the elites? How do the elites differ from the rank and file in terms of social and demographic background?

The purpose of table 6.7 is to describe the composition of the three elites compared to the rank-and-file voters. To what extent are the elite groups representative of various social strata? We shall consider five background variables: strength of party identification, gender, age, education, and occupation.

An overwhelming majority of the generalist elite and the party elite are strong party identifiers. However, more than one-third of the corporatist elite is nonpartisan. Gender variations are considerable. All elite groups are more or less male dominated. The strong overrepresentation of men in the generalist elite is surprising considering that one-third of the Storting representatives (in the period 1985–89) and nearly half of the cabinet ministers were women. The probable explanation is that a system of gender quotas is applied in the nominations for Storting elections (see chap. 5). Young voters, that is, those less than thirty years old, are consistently underrepresented in all three elite groups.

Table 6.7 does not lend much support to the widely held view that elites tend to be recruited from among the higher educated strata (Putnam, 1976). In fact, the educational level is almost identical for the party elite and the rank and file, but it is somewhat higher for the corporative and the generalist elites. Similarly, the elites are not particularly distinct concerning occupational composition. The proportion of manual workers is relatively high in all elite groups, particularly in the corporative elite. Both of these departures from expectations seem to reflect the long

Table 6.7
Social Composition of Elites vs. Non-elites (%)

	Generalist Elite	Corporative Elite	Party Elite	Rank and File	Total
Party ID					
Strong	74	33	79	35	41
Weak	20	30	17	29	28
Non-partisan	6	37	4	36	31
Gender					
Male	73	62	54	48	52
Female	27	38	46	52	48
Age					
≤ 30	7	19	19	32	28
31–50	57	57	30	33	37
> 50	36	24	51	35	35
Education					
Elementary only	18	20	32	31	29
Gymnas or equivalent (parts or completed)	55	52	53	55	64
University	27	28	15	14	17
Occupation					
Workers	31	38	25	33	33
Functionaires, public	28	30	17	14	17
Functionaires, private	14	14	19	22	20
Independents	4	5	13	10	9
Farmers, fishermen	19	6	10	3	5
Others	4	7	16	18	16
Total	100	100	100	100	100
N	100	269	217	1573	2169

dominance of Norwegian politics by the Labor Party. In the corporative and the generalist elites, functionaries in public employment are substantially overrepresented while private functionaries and independents in business are correspondingly underrepresented. Farmers and fishermen are overrepresented in all elite groups.

The data support the view that citizens' participation is mostly channeled through the party system and through nonparty organizations.

Table 6.8
Sense of Political Efficacy (% Disagreeing with Statements)

Statements	Generalist Elite	Party Elite	Corporatist Elite	Rank and File
It is difficult to see where the dividing line between parties goes	42	33	22	16
What happens in politics is rarely of any great importance to me	76	68	64	52
Politics is often so complicated that ordinary people cannot follow what it is all about	39	37	35	29
People like me can vote, but there is nothing else we can do to influence politics	64	59	55	41

Both channels are open to everybody, and roughly one-fourth of the sample has reported activity in either party or organizations or in both. In terms of social composition the activists tend to represent an average of the population, although with a slight bias, particularly for the generalist elite.

These different types of activists have different attitudes and feelings about politics and their place in it. We presented our respondents with a series of statements expressing disillusionment and helplessness in the face of the complexities of contemporary politics and asked them to agree or disagree with them. The results are presented in table 6.8. The members of the generalist elite, followed by the party elite and corporatist elite, disagreed with the statements far more often than the rank and file. The activists—especially the generalist and party elite members—have a far stronger sense of political efficacy than the inactive. Whether their activity results in these feelings, or whether these feelings lead to their political activity, we cannot say. Perhaps some mix of both is involved.

We also gave our respondents a set of statements about their trust in government and democracy (see table 6.9). Here the important finding is that the differences between the elite groups and the voters were small. A large majority of all Norwegians trust government and feel that democracy is working satisfactorily.

Table 6.9
Trust in Government (% Giving Trusting Answers)

Questions	Generalist Elite	Party Elite	Corporatist Elite	Rank and File
Do you think that those who govern are wasting a great deal of money we pay in taxes, that they waste some of it, or that they waste very little money?	84	80	71	71
Do you believe that most Norwegian politicians are competent and usually know what they are doing, or do you think that many of them lack knowledge about the matters they are supposed to deal with?	72	70	72	67
Do you think that most of our politicians are trustworthy, that politicians by and large are trustworthy, or that only a few Norwegian politicians are trustworthy?	90	90	87	84
How satisfied are you with the way democracy works in this country? Are you very satisfied, fairly satisfied, not very satisfied, or not satisfied at all?	89	89	91	89

Political Opinions

So far in this chapter we have focused mostly upon the activities of the Norwegian electorate—how much and how the members participate in political life. Now we shall look at their policy views in 1985 and how these opinions are organized.

Our 1985 interviews with the electorate contained no less than 40 questions on the respondents' feelings and opinions about the issues of the day. These were not all asked at once—few people would stand still for such a barrage—but were scattered throughout the interview. The questions were asked in several different ways; about half were statements taken from the national election dialogue with which the respondents were asked to agree or disagree and then to indicate how strong this agreement or disagreement was. The remainder of the questions contained several possible answers and the respondents were asked to choose one.

In table 6.10 we present a summary of responses to the questions and statements about issues. The opinion balance of each item is the percent in favor of the position minus the percent against. (Those favoring neither position are ignored, along with those who don't know or fail to answer at all.) These figures provide a quick view of the net popularity or unpopularity of various issue positions in 1985. NATO (69 percent), foreign aid (67 percent) , more economic growth (64 percent), more public nursery schools (62 percent), a trade boycott of South Africa (59 percent), and improving rural areas rather than big cities (44 percent) were popular. They also were government policy and had been for some time. Attempts to stop abortions (-48 percent), charges of abuse in the state welfare system (-62 percent), and a proposal to abolish grading in junior high schools (-70 percent) were unpopular. The issues seen by the electorate to be highly controversial are the ones with small opinion balances: for example, the statement that couples living together should have the same rights as married couples (11 percent), a proposal to build private hospitals (-2 percent), or a proposal to increase economic aid to immigrants (-11 percent). The readers, especially those not familiar with Norwegian politics, can learn something about Norway in the mid-1980s by browsing through this list.

Obviously, there are many issues in Norwegian politics and most Norwegians have opinions about them—but not everyone. The right column of table 6.10 indicates the percentage of the respondents who did not respond to, or said they didn't have an opinion about each question. There is a lot of variation depending upon the issue, from more than 20 percent to a trace. The average for all forty issues is 12.5 percent. This figure alone does not tell us what proportion of the Norwegian electorate is uninformed on these issues since the "don't knows" are not the same people on each issue. So we counted the frequencies with which individual respondents gave a "don't know" answer on these questions. The results are in table 6.11. Two-thirds of the respondents answered "don't know" only once, or not at all. The other third of the electorate was less well informed.

Table 6.10

Public Opinions on Controversial Issues in 1985

Type of Opinion Distribution	Issues	Opinion Balance (%)	DK/NAs (%)
A	Positive for NATO	69	5
A	Positive about development aid	67	21
A	We should rely on economic growth and higher productivity	64	9
A	We must build more *barnehager*	62	5
A	Stop trade with South Africa	59	9
A	Favor rural development over cities	44	8
A	Build public service rather than reduce taxes	43	11
A	For atom-free zone	41	27
A	Forbid all forms of pornography	40	6
A	Forbid advertising on radio/TV	40	8
C	Lower pension age rather than cut workday	34	7
C	Women should have ½ members of public boards/councils	32	4
A	Tax reduction for low-income people	31	24
C	Oil business is too complicated	27	9
C	Favor industrial development	23	10
C	Employees should have ½ of board of directors	21	9
C	Reduce state control over economic life	11	13
A	Efforts to achieve equality should be expanded	11	5
B	Couples living together have same rights as married people	11	5
B	More private firms in North Sea oil production	6	17
B	For private hospitals	−2	10
B	The oil business is very risky	−5	13
B	Reduce size of the public sector	−7	45
B	Negotiate atomic zone only through NATO	−5	13

Table 6.10

continued

Type of Opinion Distribution	Issues	Opinion Balance (%)	DK/NAs (%)
C	Increase economic aid to immigrants	−11	7
B	Reduce rate of oil/gas production	−12	19
B	Moderate, simplify government regulations	13	26
C	Create council to combat unemployment	−20	21
C	Christian teachings in elementary schools	−21	7
B	Politicians rather than experts should control oil industry	−22	8
C	Increase speed of hydroelectric power development	−24	17
C	Reduce defense spending	−28	9
A	Nationalize big business	−29	15
B	Critical of USSR's foreign policy	−30	21
C	Lower taxes on high incomes	−37	7
B	Critical of USA's foreign policy	−38	22
A	No to abortion	−48	2
B	There is much abuse in social welfare	−62	4
A	Abolish grade in junior high school	−70	6
A	There should be less social insurance	−72	16
		Avg. 12.5	

Source: Aardal and Valen (1989), 56–57, table 4.1.

*Note: N*s: A = 16, B = 12, C = 12.

Table 6.11

Frequency of Respondents Answering "Don't Know"

No. of Don't Knows	% of Respondents
0	25
1	22
2	19
3	13
4	8
5	5
6	3
7	2
8	2
9	1
10 or more	a

Note: Computed on twenty-three questions for which DKs were separately coded.

[a]Less than 0.5%.

The Distribution of Opinions

The distribution of public opinions among the citizenry is of great significance to practical politicians and analysts alike (Key, 1961: part I). The simple distribution of yes's and no's is of interest—an issue position favored by 90 percent of the electorate and opposed by 10 percent is very different from one favored by 52 percent and opposed by 48 percent. And the political opinions of electorates rarely fall neatly into just two categories but are more realistically thought of as ranging along a continuum from utterly opposed through lesser degrees of negativity to neutrality, and then through gradually increasingly positive feelings until the totally positive end of the continuum is reached. Our data allow us to look at the forty issues in table 6.11 in this way. When we do so we find several different kinds of opinion distribution.

The most common form of opinion distribution in political issues in 1985 we shall call type A. The distribution of preferences looked like the J-shaped curve in figure 6.5. A very large majority are in favor of this issue position, mostly strongly so. Support declines sharply as we look at the numbers who are neutral or negative. (Of course, if we looked at an issue very strongly opposed by the electorate, the J-shaped curve would be flip-

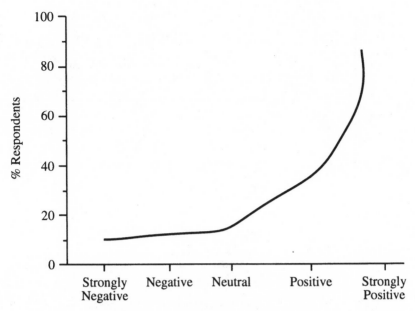

Figure 6.5 Type A Opinion Distribution

flopped.) This is the most common form of opinion distribution in Norway (or at least in the forty issues we have studied)—sixteen out of forty cases look this way (see table 6.11, first column). Feelings about NATO, development aid, economic growth, the need for nursery schools, and so on are very positive type A cases. The electorate was equally united in opposition to reductions in social welfare benefits, abolishing grading in schools, and forbidding abortions. The A cases display high consensus. Type A positive issues are usually government policy, and those that aren't probably will be soon. Type A negative distributions are less frequent and tend to fade away, unless the small minority of positives are organized and adamant about keeping the issue on the agenda. A good example is anti-abortion activists. There is not much serious conflict in this type of situation.

Opinion distributions in Norway take two additional forms. Type B issue distributions approximate a normal distribution, bell-shaped curve (see fig. 6.6). Here the bulk of the opinions are in the middle while both the political extremes are small. There is more conflict than in type A cases, but large coalitions tend to be moderate. The way politicians and parties try to garner votes is by moving to the center. Real-life opinion distributions are messier than the ideal, but approximately twelve of the

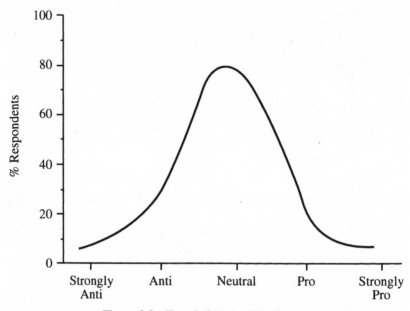

Figure 6.6 Type B Opinion Distribution

forty issues are classified as type B. Among these issues are those concerning the legal rights of cohabiting couples, private hospitals, and the size of the public sector (see table 6.11, left column).

The most conflictual issues we classify as type C (fig. 6.7). Here there is more than one mode; in our idealized example there are two. These modes tend to be at or near the extremes; the middle of the distribution is weak, and the possibility of sharp conflict is high. None of the forty issues we studied was as sharply U-shaped as the idealized curve, but approximately twelve opinion distributions have two or more modes and relatively few persons with moderate views. Some of these high-conflict issues are tax reductions (on high incomes), defense spending, immigration policy, and teaching Christianity in the schools.

Norwegian opinion distributions on public issues, at least in 1985, were mostly consensual or moderately conflictual. The reasons for this are not altogether clear, although the absence of religious and racial conflicts certainly is a contributing factor. And Norwegian political institutions and practices seem to have rewarded consensus-building over the principled pursuit of non-negotiable goals. The leaders of the Labor Party, after a brief flirtation with Marxist-Leninism (in the 1920s) opted

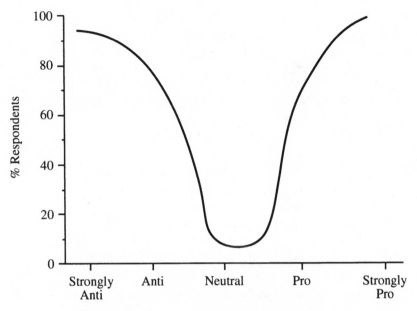

Figure 6.7 Type C Opinion Distribution

for social democracy; the Conservatives abandoned their initial opposition to social democracy for the argument that they could run the welfare state more efficiently and fairly than Labor. Policy ideas that would be deeply divisive are avoided, if possible. Few issues have deeply divided Norway for a long time; the nation's relationship with Europe is the best recent case of one that has. Type C issues may be rare, but they portend the greatest possibility of large changes in public policy or in the political system.

Political Belief Systems

A second way of looking at the political opinions of Norwegians is to examine how these opinions relate to one another. If the respondents' answers to questions about policy tend to cluster together, and one can accurately predict how they will stand on issue B from their position on issue A, then the respondents' political views are organized into a belief system or ideology. An electorate whose members consider each issue separately on its merit and without concern for how they react to other issues probably does not exist in the real world. Ideologies allow politicians and electors to make decisions wholesale by lumping numerous, complex issues into one: is this a liberal or conservative proposal, a social democratic or free enterprise plan, a feminist or a male chauvinist idea, and so on.

Bernt Aardal and Henry Valen (1989: chap. 4) have empirically studied the structure of Norwegian political opinions since 1969 using factor analysis. They found four ideological dimensions in 1985. The most important of these dimensions, made up of responses to fourteen questions, they called Official Control v. Private Initiative. (Questions on defense issues also fell into this dimension.) The second-largest factor or dimension was entitled Welfare, Caring, Equality and contained nine issue questions. The third dimension contained four issues concerned with Morality and Religion. The fourth dimension concerned Growth and Energy.

This way of organizing opinions can and does change over time. The first dimension, Official Control v. Private Initiative, has been the dominant issue dimension among the Norwegian electorate at least since 1969. The moral-religious dimension has been stable over time. Other issue dimensions have waxed and waned (Aardal and Valen 1989: 63).

Conclusions

What are the represented like in Norway? They are not, on the average, very interested or informed or active in politics. Despite this, they do vote in parliamentary elections in large numbers. This undermotivated voting suggests strong pro-voting norms and institutions that can mobilize the disinterested enough to get them to the polls. The party system appears to perform this function. Those Norwegians who identify with any one of the parties tend to be regular voters no matter what their interest level is. More demanding activities—joining parties, writing to newspapers, contacting elected officials—are rare. Despite this picture, the represented seem to be satisfied with the performance of their institutions, including the Storting.

A minority—somewhere between 10 and 20 percent—of Norwegians are active, interested, and informed about political affairs. This is a largely self-chosen elite open to anyone. We identify three different sets of activists—the party elite, the corporative elite, and the generalist elite. The party elite are the dues-paying members of parties who are not active in private associations; the corporative elite are active members of private associations who are not party members; and the generalist elite are those active in both arenas. These are the men and women who make up the real audience for most political debate, who fill the party offices, who attend party meetings at local and provincial levels. Interestingly, these elites are not very different from other Norwegians. They are more often middle-aged males, but their educational levels are not much different from those of everyone else—especially in the case of the party elite—and the proportion of manual workers is surprisingly high. The activist elites have happier feelings about Norwegian politics and government and are less apt to lapse into cynicism and distrust.

The represented in Norway tend to be much more opinionated than active. We have described those opinions in some detail above. The most common distribution of opinions in Norway (sixteen of the issues we studied in 1985) is highly consensual. Most people were strongly on the same side of the issue. Frequently, these opinions have already been embodied in law; those which have not are likely candidates to become government policy. When this heavy consensus is lined up against some one issue or proposal, that issue or proposal is likely to disappear from the agenda quickly. (The major exception would be issues with strong institutionalized support.)

The second kind of opinion distribution—approximately twelve of the forty issues—approximates the bell-shaped normal distribution curve. There is more conflict about these issues, but that conflict tends to be moderated by the fact that more people are in the middle than at the extremes of the political scene. The third opinion distribution on political issues is the most conflictual. Here there are two or more modes, and the centrist positions are scarce. We classify twelve of the forty issues as being of this type.

In sum, the represented in Norway are not deeply divided by seemingly irreconcilable conflicts—usually racial or religious—that embitter the politics of so many other countries. But there are conflicts of opinion within Norway's represented. In 1985, we find that the issues could be usefully arrayed along four issue dimensions. The largest of these and the most stable was government control v. private initiative. Next were conflicts over welfare, caring, and equality, morality and religion, and growth and energy.

No doubt members of the contemporary Storting are sometimes staggered by the number and complexity of the issues that come before them. But compared to representatives in many, perhaps most, other countries, they have it fairly easy.

7

Political Parties

Political parties are a prominent feature of the Norwegian scene. The nation's press depicts politics largely in terms of competition between the parties. Public opinion polls regularly report on their current popularity and future prospects. The names and faces of national party leaders are nearly as well known as those of sports stars, pop singers, and television personalities. On election day Norwegians vote for—and against—political parties, not directly for individual candidates.

All of this is thought to facilitate the process of representative democracy. By narrowing and focusing the choice of candidates and issues, by campaigning for these people and programs, and by then seeing that electoral promises are carried out by winners, political parties provide an essential link between voters and public officials. This is the party mandate theory of policy representation we outlined in chapter 1. But systematic efforts to examine whether political parties actually perform these functions are rare. In this chapter we shall look at the Norwegian parties to see how closely they conform to the party mandate model.

Party Competition

For the party mandate model to work, voters must have a choice between parties—there must be party competition. Norwegian party politics has been competitive since the battles between Venstre and Høyre began in the 1870s and 1880s. Since the end of World War II, from five to seven parties have regularly elected members to the Storting. The division of the vote between them is presented in figure 7.1. Clearly the Labor Party has been the dominant factor in Norwegian electoral politics since 1945. For a time some concern was expressed—with only a touch of hyperbole—that Norway was becoming a one-party state (Seip, 1963). But Labor has not won a majority of the vote since 1957 and seems to be declin-

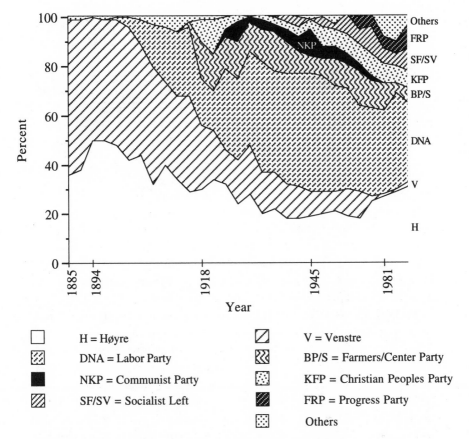

Figure 7.1 Partisan Distribution of Votes in Storting Elections, 1885–1989. *Sources:* Heidar (1983), 128–29, table 4.2; Torp (1990), 193.

ing in electoral strength along with social democratic parties everywhere. No other party seems likely to achieve majority status in the foreseeable future. Proportional representation elections, a low threshold to overcome before winning a seat in Parliament, and state-funded electoral campaigns have reduced the costs of starting new political parties and thus increased the difficulty of aggregating majority support. The proliferation of new and vexing issues since the 1970s has resulted in much electoral volatility.

It is possible, however, for the parties to be competitive at the national level but not to offer realistic party alternatives in individual electoral districts. This would seem to be a special danger in a state like Norway with a strong regional cast to its politics and electoral districts fixed by the

Constitution. The party mandate model of representation cannot work well if the voters have little chance of changing the parties, and hence the people, in their fylke's delegation to the Storting.

Party competition at the fylke level is less robust than it is nationally. There are many ways to measure party competition, but perhaps the most appropriate way for present purposes is to equate competitiveness with the ability to win seats in Parliament. If a constituency party consistently fails to elect members it is not offering much of an alternative to the voters. The Norwegian parties vary widely in this respect. The two largest political parties—the Labor Party and Høyre—competed successfully in all nineteen electoral districts in the elections of 1973, 1977, and 1981. The Christian People's Party came the next closest to being a national electoral force during this same period, but it won no seats at all in three fylker. The Center Party won no seats in four districts, the Socialist Left in eight, the Progress Party in nine, and Venstre lost out entirely in sixteen. This is not just discouraging to the local party activists, it also denies voters a full range of parties to vote for that might win a seat.

In table 7.1 we show the number of seats each electoral district has, the number of parties winning at least one of those seats, and the highest percentage of the total vote received by a single party in the three national elections held during the 1973–81 period. While there are important regional differences in the strength of the parties, there are no areas in which a single party dominates as in "the solid South" in the United States (no longer solidly Democratic) or in heavily Labor or Tory constituencies in Britain. Only infrequently does a Norwegian party poll a majority of the votes cast in a fylke; usually there are two, three, or four additional parties with whom it must share the delegation. All other things being equal, the fylker with the largest number of seats to fill tend to provide the best opportunities for the smaller parties—the correlation between the number of seats in the fylke's delegation and the number of parties it elects representatives from is +.76. The southwestern fylker tend to have more, and more evenly matched, parties than elsewhere. On the whole there seems to be enough competition between the parties at the fylke level to meet the conditions of the party government model fairly well.

However, party competition in Norway is multiparty competition. None of the current political parties except Labor has polled a majority or won a majority of the seats in Parliament in the modern era. None of them, including Labor, is likely to do so in the foreseeable future. This means that no Norwegian party faces the prospect of implementing a legislative program without the cooperation of at least one other party with

Table 7.1

Competitiveness of Political Parties by Fylke, 1973–1981

Fylke	No. of Seats	No. of Parties Winning 1 or More Seats	Highest % of Vote Received by a Single Party
Østfold	8	4	51 (DNA)
Akershus	10	7	40 (DNA)
Oslo	15	5	43 (H)
Hedmark	8	4	60 (DNA)
Oppland	7	4	56 (DNA)
Buskerud	7	5	49 (DNA)
Vestfold	7	4	42 (H)
Telemark	6	4	50 (H)
Aust-Agder	4	3	39 (DNA)
Vest-Agder	5	4	30 (DNA)
Rogaland	10	5	34 (H)
Hordaland	15	7	36 (H)
Sogn og Fjordane	5	4	32 (DNA)
Møre og Romsdal	10	6	32 (DNA)
Sør-Trøndelag	10	6	45 (DNA)
Nord-Trøndelag	6	3	46 (DNA)
Nordland	12	3	46 (DNA)
Troms	6	5	45 (DNA)
Finnmark	4	3	55 (DNA)

its own distinctive legislative program. The translation of voter preferences into legislative decisions is thus not as simple or as straightforward as in the party mandate model. The policy consequences of electoral outcomes depends upon pre- and/or post-election negotiations conducted in the process of forming coalition governments, or in seeking the additional votes a one-party minority government needs in order to do anything in Parliament. Under these conditions then, party mandates are somewhat conditional—none of the parties can carry out its pledges alone.

Party Manifestos

Norwegian political parties spend much time, energy, and emotion debating public issues within their own ranks until they arrive at a party platform or electoral manifesto upon which their candidates are expected to campaign. These documents are usually quite extensive, over fifty pages in length. The predictability of Norwegian calendar elections facilitates preparation of such elaborate policy statements. Not many people actually read the manifestos, but they are significant anyway. The process of preparing and adopting the statements is a learning experience at least for the activists involved. The finished product guides the behavior of party leaders, candidates, and the news media.

Agreement and Disagreement between Parties

It is not enough, according to the theory of party government, that political parties espouse policies—the policies must differ. Kaare Strøm and Jørn Leipart's (1989) content analysis of Norwegian party manifestos since World War II addresses this question. Methodologically, their article replicates Ian Budge, David Robertson, and Derek Hearl's (1987) study of party electoral programs in nineteen other Western democracies. Both studies take a saliency approach—the frequency with which topics are mentioned in a party's manifesto is assumed to indicate their importance to that party. These frequencies were factor analyzed to yield spatial representations of the policy positions of the parties.

The Norwegian analysis finds a strong left-right social welfare policy dimension in the party platforms. Several other weaker dimensions also were identified from the analysis, the most important being a moral-religious dimension. This picture of the dimensions of partisan conflict is much the same as that emerging from Norwegian voting studies (see chap. 2 and the literature cited therein, chap. 6). But two of Strøm and Leipart's findings break new ground.

First, they point out sizable areas of policy agreement between the parties. All of the manifestos—including even the libertarian Progress Party's—ranked expansion of the welfare state among their top ten goals (271). Indeed, most of the parties agreed with each other on what the top ten issues were. Party conflict in Norway is thus muted by large areas of agreement. Perhaps total partisan conflict would be more dangerous to Norwegian democracy than limited conflict combined with large areas of agreement (Eckstein, 1966). Whether one accepts this interpretation or not, it seems to be an accurate depiction of Norwegian realities.

A second Strøm and Leipart finding of special relevance to this study is that the Norwegian party platforms gradually converged from 1949 until the 1970s (figure 7.2). This strong tendency to reduce the differences

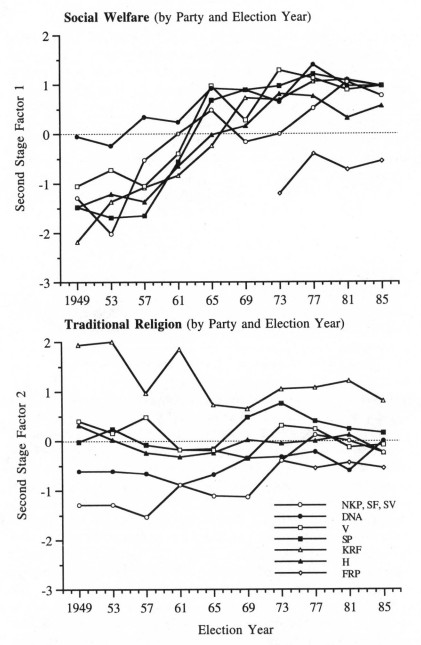

Figure 7.2 Ideological Positions of Norwegian Parties as Reflected in Election Manifestos. *Source:* Strøm and Leipart (1989), figs. 1, 2.

between the parties can be interpreted in a variety of ways. It can be seen as a reflection of changing attitudes among voters: as the Labor Party dominated the direction of public policy in the 1950s and 1960s everyone became a social democrat. Or it can be interpreted as a rational response of losing political parties that want to win: a "matching strategy" in Anthony Downs's vocabulary or a "moving consensus" in V. O. Key's terms (Downs, 1957; Key, 1958: 243–49). No matter what you call it, the established Norwegian parties moved toward the center and the positions of the Labor Party during the last half century. As the policy differences between the established parties became more blurred two new parties—the Socialist Left and the Progress Party—came into being to represent the extremes of the political spectrum. Party differences on policy matters are not constant but change over the decades.

Manifestos and the Voters

We have looked in more detail at the party manifestos for the 1985 election, comparing them with the policy preferences of voters as measured by the national election study of that same year. In table 7.2 the positions of the parties on these issues are summarized. The first thing we might point out is the consensus (or near consensus) on a number of issues. A strong defense, more equality between the sexes, more environmental protection, and aid to developing countries were favored by all, or all but one, of the party manifestos. Other issues were more controversial. Some of these were long-standing areas of controversy upon which the parties have well-known positions: the socialist parties' commitment to social equality, the Christian People's Party's concern for Christian faith and morality, the Center Party's support for the rural periphery, the Conservative and Progress Parties' belief in capitalism and free markets. These are the central issues that have defined the parties for decades. The parties can try to redefine what these commitments mean under today's circumstances, but otherwise they have little room (and usually no desire) to change.

Finally, there are the newer issues and controversies, things such as child care, or immigration, or the role of private medical doctors and hospitals in the nation's health system. Judging from the manifestos, the parties tend to approach these issues cautiously and to take moderate, or highly qualified, or highly unclear positions on them.

In order to look at the connection between the 1985 party manifestos and the preferences of party voters, we computed a party agreement

Table 7.2

1985 Party Manifestos

Issue	Strong, Explicit ++ Pro	Weak, Inferred + Pro	None 0 Both/And	Weak, Inferred − Con	Strong, Explicit −− Con
Maintain strong defense	DNA SP H FrP	KrF			SV
Sexual equality	SV DNA SP H	KrF	FrP		
Abolition of grades	DNA	SV	SP		FrP KrF H
Christian faith and morals	SP KrF	H	DNA		SV FrP
Social equality	SV DNA	SP KrF	H FrP		
Ban on nuclear weapons	SV DNA	SP KrF	H		FrP

continued

Table 7.2
continued

Issue	Strong, Explicit ++	Weak, Inferred +	None 0	Weak, Inferred −	Strong, Explicit −−
	Pro		Both/And	Con	
Lower taxes	H FrP	SP KrF	SV DNA		
Lower interest on housing loans	SV DNA	SP KrF	H FrP		
Support peripheral regions	SP KrF		SV DNA H	FrP	
End state regulation of business	FrP H			SP KrF	SV DNA
Environmental protection	SV DNA SP KrF H	FrP			

Aid to developing countries	SV DNA SP KrF H				FrP
Stop growth in public expenditures	H FrP		KrF	DNA SP	SV
Prohibit private hospitals	SV DNA		SP H	KrF	FrP
Expand public sector to achieve full employment	SV DNA	SP	KrF		H FrP
Strengthen cities	SV DNA H	SP KrF	FrP		
Day care	SV DNA	SP H	KrF		FrP
Make immigration more difficult	FrP	SP	H KrF		SV DNA

Table 7.3

Party Agreement Scores of Voters by Position of
Their Party's Manifesto 1985

Party's Manifesto Position	Mean Party Agreement Score of Party Voters
Strongly pro	+44
Moderately, unclearly, implicitly pro	−2
No position, yes and no	−6
Moderately, unclearly, implicitly con	−2
Strongly con	−37

Note: Party Agreement Score = (% of party voters agreeing with their party's manifesto) − (% of party voters disagreeing with manifesto).

score for the voters of each party for each issue. This measure is simply the percentage of a party's voters agreeing with an issue position minus the percentage disagreeing. A score of 100 represents complete agreement and 0 represents total disagreement. (The sign of the score indicates direction.) We then averaged the agreement scores of all the parties on all issues on which they took a strong positive position in their manifestos, a moderate positive position, no position, a moderate negative position, and a strong negative position. These average or mean scores are presented in table 7.3. The 1985 results are clear: When Norwegian parties took a strong position in their manifestos either for or against a policy, the average party agreement score indicated moderate agreement with the position by party voters. But when party manifestos took moderate or unclear positions, the average party unity scores indicated nearly complete disagreement among party voters. Party manifestos, at least in 1985, reflect or shape opinion within the parties to some degree.

But this is by no means automatic. There are numerous and interesting departures from the overall trend. For example, the 1985 Labor Party manifesto advocated an end to the grading of children in the secondary schools. The proposal proved to be unpopular, even to most Labor voters. The same manifesto committed the party to maintaining a strong national defense, but there was little agreement on this among rank-and-file Labor voters. The Progress Party's manifesto opposed more public day care centers, while Progress voters strongly favored them. And so on.

Party manifestos do seem to provide a loose linkage between the party activists who write them and the voters. But there is plenty of disagreement about policy within the parties and agreement on policy between parties. The voting cues that the Norwegian parties provide are crystal clear on some issues—usually issues which have been around for decades. On newer issues the parties are vague, thereby providing less policy guidance to voters when they are most likely to need it.

Core Issues

Each political party in Norway has a few issues upon which it agrees. On other matters there is less consensus and sometimes considerable conflict within the ranks. As an illustration, examine table 7.4. Here the index of agreement of all 1985 Labor voters is arranged from the issues they agreed upon most—a commitment to social welfare programs, an active government, and economic growth—to campaign issues that divided the party down the middle—defense expenditures, issues concerning oil and gas production, immigration, and the nationalization of big business. Arrays for the other parties show a similar pattern—a few issues with scores in the 80s and 90s, balanced by others about which there is little or no agreement. Only 9 percent of all the indices of agreement scores for all the parties are 80 and above. We shall call these areas of general agreement within the party core issues.

These core issues are well known. The Socialist Left shares a concern for the welfare state with Labor, but wants more, faster. Foreign policy opposition led to the split of Labor in 1961 and to the establishment of the neutralist Socialist People's Party. In 1972 this party formed an election alliance with the Communists and a splinter group from Labor over the EC issue. This alliance subsequently turned into the Socialist Left Party, which has stressed opposition to NATO, the U.S., and atomic weapons ever since. The Socialist Left has a high degree of consensus on women's issues—abortion rights, child care, and so on. The Labor Party has dominated Norwegian politics since 1935 with its commitment to a thoroughgoing and generous welfare state. Jobs has been another preoccupation, leading to an emphasis on economic growth at least in the party's rhetoric. The core issues of the Liberals used to be the democratization of the political system. These objectives having been largely achieved, Venstre has been without a clear set of core issues. In recent elections, it has emphasized environmental protection (Aardal, 1990). The Christian People's Party should not be confused with Christian parties elsewhere in Europe (Karvonen, 1993). It is a party committed to the protection of Christian values and morality. The Center Party is a direct lineal

Table 7.4

Index of Agreement, Labor Party Voters, 1985

Statement/Question	Index of Agreement	Direction
Decrease social welfare/insurance programs	81	−
Stress economic growth and productivity	70	+
Social welfare programs lead to abuse	67	−
Public services more important than tax reduction	67	+
Create more nursery schools	66	+
Against trade with South Africa	65	+
In favor of aid to developing countries	65	+
Abolish grades in junior high school	62	−
In favor of NATO	62	+
No to abortion	60	−
Lower taxes on high incomes	56	−
Workers ought to elect ½ of boards of directors of private concerns	54	+
In favor of private health services	54	−
Women should be ½ of official committees and cabinet	50	+
Forbid all forms of pornography	48	+
Favor the countryside over the cities	46	+
Christian instruction in nursing schools	32	−
In favor of reduction of public sector	30	−
Allow advertising on radio/TV	30	+
Continue industrial expansion	27	+
More private firms in North Sea oil production	24	−
Public economic steering to avoid unemployment	23	+
Equality ought to be more widespread	22	+
Living together is as correct as marriage	19	+
Increase development of waterways	17	−
Reduce state control of business	15	−
Reduce defense expenditures	12	−
Reduce rate of oil and gas production	12	−
Monetary support for the culture of immigrants	11	−
Nationalize big businesses	8	+
Too much risk in oil drilling	4	−

Table 7.5

Rank Order of Selected Questions by Party Voters, 1985 Election

Question/Issues	SV	DNA	V	KrF	SP	H	FrP
Health care	1	1	2	1	1	1	1
Care for the aged	2	2	5.5	4	2	2	3
Employment	5	3	5.5	8	7	8	5.5
Control of atomic weapons	3	6	4	a	10	a	9
Social equalization	6	5	a	a	9	a	a
Control of government	a	7	a	a	5	9	10
Energy/environment	9	a	1	a	4	a	a
Defense	7	10	3	9	a	5	9
Taxes	a	a	a	a	a	4	2
Preschooling (*barnehager*)	8	9	9	5	a	a	a
Size of public section	a	a	a	a	a	10	8
Social issues	4	4	a	7	8	a	6
Other economic issues	a	a	a	a	a	3	4

[a]Not ranked in top ten questions/issues.

descendant of the Farmers' Party; its core issues are the protection of rural life, subsidies for farmers, and decentralization. The Conservatives are pro-business and believe in free markets and laissez-faire. Once strongly opposed to the welfare state, Høyre has learned to accept the inevitable and now stresses cost containment, efficiency, and equity in welfare programs. The Progress Party is, in part, a response to the Conservative Party's acceptance of the welfare state—it stresses far right economics, suspicions of the state, and opposition to immigration.

Party voters not only tend to agree upon core issues, they also tend to consider their core issues of special importance. In 1985, the voters were asked an open-ended question after the election about the most important issues or problems in the campaign. When the responses are looked at by party, we see that party voters tend to see their party's core issues as more important than other voters do (table 7.5). The voters in all the parties save one saw health care as the No. 1 issue in 1985. The one exception were the Liberal voters who ranked health care second, after their core issue of the environment. The Socialist Left voters thought control of atomic weapons more important than the voters of any other party. Labor voters put welfare and employment at the top of their list. The Christians saw abortion, family policy, and various issues related to instruction in the schools as especially important, far more important than anyone else.

Table 7.6

Mean Index of Agreement, by Party Level

	SV	DNA	V	SP	KrF	H	FrP
Members of Storting (18 issues)	73.9	63.7	a	61	64.3	56.9	a
Party activists (17 issues)	84.1	65.9	65.0	48.5	47.8	51.9	65.5
Party voters (31 issues)	52.1	40.6	43.8	37.8	41.2	44.5	38.6

[a]Too few cases.

The Center Party voters were the only group to list decentralization as an important issue. The Conservatives and the Progress Party felt economic issues—especially taxes and inflation—were more important than other voters did. This tendency to consider core issues more important than others reduces the significance of disagreements on issues within the parties; after all, the partisans agree on "the important things."

So far we have looked only at agreement and disagreement among party voters. Let us expand our attention to include party activists and members of the Storting. As can be seen in table 7.6, both of these groups tend to agree on policy issues more than the ordinary voters of their own parties. This, perhaps, is not surprising. In order to become a member of the Storting a person must be (or at least appear to be) a reliable and trustworthy party figure; those who stray far from the party line seldom pass the test. Our group of party activists are quite experienced politicians, many of them local, elected public officials. Both Storting members and party activists live in a highly politicized world; almost all voters do not. Thus the greater agreement of Storting members and activists is understandable. However, the implications of this for policy representation are less clear.

All the parties represent their own voters well on some issues. These core issues can change over time, but since this involves changing the attitudes of larger numbers of inattentive and disinterested people, they do so slowly. Thus new issues do not quickly and easily become core issues. There is a tendency for the parties to represent the past better than the future. Thus how representative a party is depends on the agenda. If a party's core issues (or matters closely related thereto) are being debated in Parliament, it can speak for the absent others with assurance. If other policy areas are at the fore, the legislative party must act even if there is no consensus among its supporters, and the party's claim to being representative is weak.

Leaders, Issues, and Parties

The party government model assumes that people vote for parties for policy reasons. We shall examine this assumption now.

At least since the publication of *The American Voter* (Campbell et al., 1960), students of voting have considered the voters' attitudes or orientations towards issues, candidates, and parties in their efforts to understand and explain voter choice. The relative importance of these variables is obvious to anyone studying policy representation. Let us look at each of the variables separately and then consider their relative importance.

Party Leaders and the Vote

Elections to the Storting have become national events, not just nineteen separate constituency elections. It is safe to assume—as most local party activists do as they laboriously put together complexly balanced lists—that the local candidates make some difference in electoral outcomes (see chap. 5). But increasingly, Storting election campaigns are dominated by national party leaders—potential prime ministers—and national issues. (The campaigns of 1981 and 1985 became "The Gro and Kaare Show," after Gro Harlem Brundtland and Kaare Willoch) This nationalization of parliamentary elections has occurred in most other countries, the apparent result of technological change, especially the influence of television. In Norway it results in an electorate that knows a handful of national leaders as well as or better than their local Storting members.

The relationship between the Norwegian voters' feelings about the party leaders and their vote in 1985 is shown in figure 7.3. Here the respondents in our sample were asked to rate the party leaders on a "feeling thermometer," a 0 to 100 scale with 100 representing complete sympathy. Clearly the more sympathetic the voters found leaders, the more likely they were to vote for his or her party—or those who vote for a party tend to develop warm feelings about its leader.

But a leader's popularity does not always translate into a vote for his or

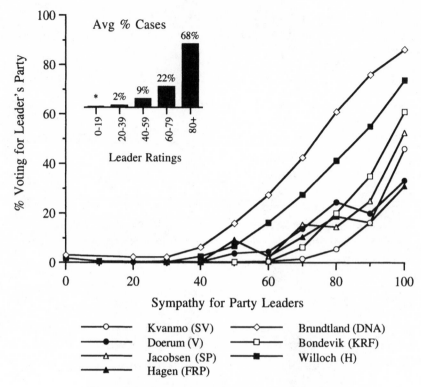

Figure 7.3   Sympathy for Leaders and 1985 Vote

her party (or vice-versa). Only 24 percent of all those rating the colorful Hanna Kvanmo of the Socialist Left very highly (a score of 90 or above) voted for her in 1985. Half the voters who rated Kvanmo that highly voted for Labor and Gro Harlem Brundtland (tables 7.7 and 7.8).

The same tendency can be seen for the leaders of the other small parties. Kjell Magne Bondevik of the Christian People's Party was a popular leader within his own party, but only half of those rating him over 90 voted for him. A quarter of those who liked him a lot voted Conservative. The flamboyant (at least by Norwegian standards) Carl I. Hagen was rated over 90 by quite a few voters, but fewer than one-third voted for him, and more than half voted for Høyre. Odd Einar Doerum, the leader of the imploding Liberals, was not very popular anywhere but had more supporters in the Labor Party than in his own. Not surprisingly, a party leader's popularity outside his or her party tends to be greatest in parties located near his or her party ideologically.

Table 7.7

How Voters Rating a Party Leader at 90+ Voted in 1985 (%)

Party Leader Rated 90+	SV	DNA	V	KrF	SP	H	FrP	Total %	N
Kvanmo (SV)	24	51	5	3	5	12	1	100	343
Brundtland (DNA)	4	90	0	1	1	3	1	100	301
Doerum (V)	15	44	26	0	15	0	0	100	27
Bondevik (KrF)	1	10	1	49	12	26	1	100	194
Jacobsen (SP)	2	7	4	18	37	30	2	100	158
Willoch (H)	.5	10	.5	10	6	68	5	100	383
Hagen (FrP)	2	11	1	3	3	52	31	100	194

Table 7.8

Party Leaders Ratings by 1985 Vote (%)

Party Leader Rated 90+	SV	DNA	V	KrF	SP	H	FrP
Kvanmo (SV)	77	32	49	5	12	9	5
Brundtland (DNA)	10	50	0	2	2	2	3
Doerum (V)	4	2	21	0	3	0	0
Bondevik (KrP)	2	3	8	54	18	11	5
Jacobsen (SP)	4	2	15	16	45	10	5
Willoch (H)	2	7	5	21	17	56	32
Hagen (FrP)	2	2	3	2	2	12	51
Total	100	100	100	100	100	100	100
N	107	547	39	177	129	464	63

The pattern is different for the leaders of the two major parties. Gro Harlem Brundtland and Kaare Willoch were less popular outside their own parties and more popular within than the small party leaders. Perhaps leading a party with little or no chance of becoming a governing party anytime soon provides opportunities to develop personal popularity that leaders of larger parties do not have.

One final point needs to be made: few Norwegians vote for a party whose leaders they dislike. A closer look at figure 7.3 shows that only about 10 percent of the electorate voted for a party whose leader they rated under 60 on the feeling thermometer. Thus while a leader's unpopularity may lead to a loss of votes, leader popularity does not invariably translate into votes for a leader's party.

Contemporary Issues and the Vote

Respondents in the 1985 election study were given a list of nine issue areas and asked which party's (or parties') policies were closest to their own preferences in each area. The percentage of the time they mentioned a party as closest to themselves provides a measure of how close voters feel to the different parties on public policy matters. The relationship between this measure and the vote is presented in figure 7.4. Predictably there is a strong positive association: people tend to vote for parties whose issue positions are perceived as being similar to their own. But not many voters are able to compare their attitudes to party policies on many issue areas. This means that the party vote was made up of a large number of voters who did not feel close to their party on many contemporary issues. In table 7.9, we look at how close voters feel to the party they voted for on issues. Almost 60 percent of those who voted for Venstre, the Christian People's Party, the Center Party, or the Progress Party in 1985 did not feel close to the party they voted for on contemporary issues. Compare this with the feelings of those who voted for Labor, the Conservatives, or the Socialist Left—large majorities of these voters felt in step with their party on issues. This does not necessarily mean that these parties are more issue oriented than the others. A more likely explanation may be found in the character of the issues included, which largely relate to the ideological left-right dimension. The policies of Labor, the Socialist Left, and the Conservatives most clearly reflect this dimension.

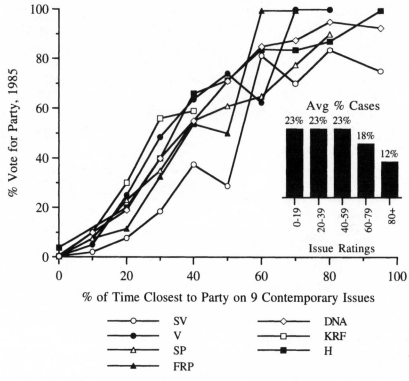

Figure 7.4 Closeness to Party on Contemporary Issues and 1985 Vote

Table 7.9
Party Voters Who Did Not Feel
Close on Issues to the Party They
Voted For, 1985

Party Voters	%
Socialist Left	30
Labor	28
Liberal	63
Christian People's	57
Center	59
The Right	25
Progress Party	65

Note: A rating below 40 on the feeling
thermometer was considered to be
"not feeling close."

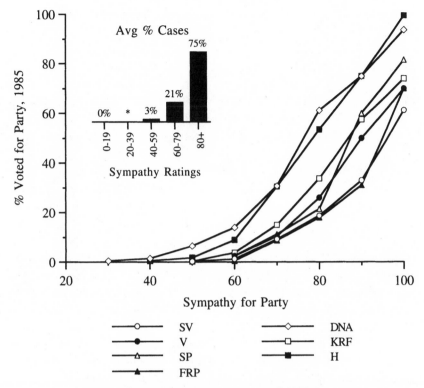

Figure 7.5 Sympathy for Parties and 1985 Vote

Political Parties and the Vote

Not surprisingly, voters tend to vote for parties with which they sympathize; the stronger the sympathy, the greater the probability they will do so (figure 7.5). Again we find that the two largest parties lead the way in translating positive feelings into votes: at the same level of approval Labor and the Conservatives achieve ten to fifteen percentage points more votes than the smaller parties do. The smaller parties, as well as their leaders, are more popular than their vote totals suggest. This gap may be the result of strategic voting—voting for one of the larger parties even though preferring one of the smaller ones.

What does this analysis tell us about the party mandate model's assumption of issue voting?

Issue voting there is in Norway. But issue voting, as used in the party mandate model, assumes a level of political knowledge about current issues that only a minority of voters possess. This severely limits the direct effects of contemporary issues on election results in a typical Norwegian election.

On the other hand, most Norwegians have fairly strong favorable feelings about the party they vote for and its national leader. These two variables are highly correlated with one another as well as with the vote. The simple correlation of feelings about a party and feelings about its leader ranges from +.71 within the Socialist Left Party to +.99 within the Progress Party.[1] Since party leaders can and do change fairly frequently without major changes in party popularity, it seems safe to assume that feelings about party shape feelings about party leaders far more than the reverse. Thus, one is led to the conclusion that (at least in 1985) feelings about the parties determined votes more than contemporary issues or the popularity or unpopularity of party leaders.

But where does sympathy for a party come from? What does it mean? Presumably it comes from the party's past performance—the leaders it has provided, the causes it has espoused, its achievements—and the voters' evaluation of that performance. A good case can be made that these retrospective judgments are a more reliable basis for rational voting decisions than estimates of party performance in an unknown future (Downs, 1957; Key, 1966; Fiorina, 1981). "Promises, promises" are the stuff of future-oriented issue voting. Judgments and feelings based upon past performance (or lack thereof) are at the heart of the Norwegian voters' feelings towards their parties, and favorite leaders as well.

How Representative Are the Parties?

Now that we have examined a number of the assumptions of the party mandate model, we turn to a more direct test of its validity: a comparison of the policy preferences of members of the Storting with the preferences of their respective parties' voters.

In figure 7.6 the average (mean) scores of members of the Storting, of the party activists who nominated them, and of the voters who voted for them are compared, by party, for eight broad issues. (We include the party activists as well as voters because of their special role in choosing parliamentary candidates.) The picture is rather different from one issue to the next.

The first issue—reducing state regulation of the economy—is an old perennial. The parties line up along the left-right axis as we would expect them to do, although they are not quite so polarized as on the other two

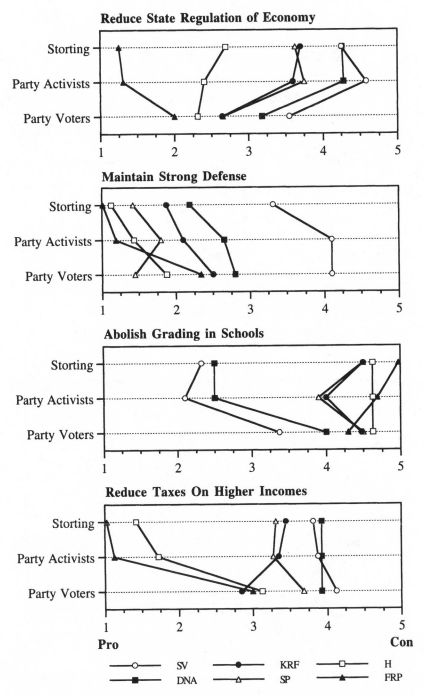

Figure 7.6 Mean Scale Scores on Policy Issues, Storting Members, Party Activists, and Voters, by Party and Issue (*continued*)

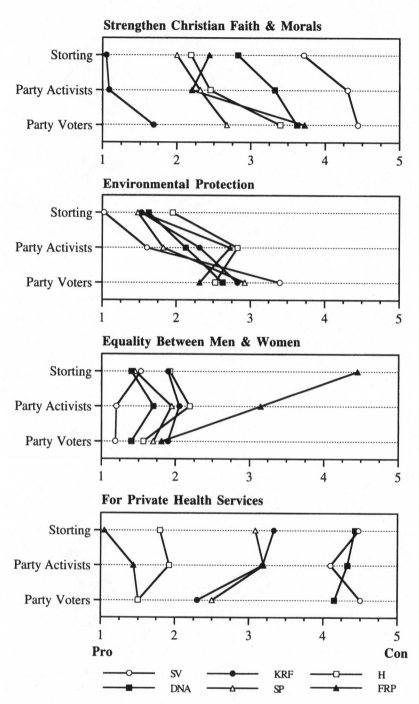

Figure 7.6 *(continued)*

economic issues examined below. The Storting members and the party activists tend to be more extreme on this issue than the party rank and file, which tend toward middling positions. On the second issue, national defense, the party rank-and-file voters seem to disagree more and the Storting members somewhat less than on economics. For all parties except the Center, the Storting members were more committed to a strong national defense than their voters. The third issue we examined concerns the proposal to abolish grading in the schools. While popular with the far left in the Socialist Left Party and the Labor Party, it was strongly opposed by everyone else, including most of their fellow partisans. A proposal to reduce taxes on higher income persons was opposed by just about everyone but the Storting members and party activists in the Conservative and Progress Parties. They took extremely favorable positions while the voters in their parties were in the indecisive middle.

The Christian People's Party raison d'être is the enhancement of Christian faith and morality. All three levels of the party are strongly in favor of such policies; the Socialist Left is nearly as united in opposition. All the other parties are in the muddled middle, although Storting members tend to be a little more favorable than the voters. Environmental protection is a relatively new issue, the voters seem to be clustered in the middle of the spectrum on it with the Storting members, almost regardless of party, being favorably inclined. Equalization of the opportunities and status of the sexes has been a major theme of Norwegian politics in recent decades, and all the parties are firmly united on the issue except the Progress Party. The Progress Party leadership is strongly opposed, while rank-and-file attitudes on the issue are similar to those found in the Conservative, Christian, and Center parties. Finally, proposals to encourage private hospitals and other health services were hotly debated in the 1985 election campaign and resulted in highly polarized opinions within the electorate along partisan lines—Storting members, activists, and voters were in agreement in all the parties.

What generalizations can be drawn from all this detail? Let us not forget that we have studied only eight issues. If a different set of issues had been chosen our results might not be the same. Also remember that we are comparing attitudes, not behavior. How members of the Storting vote on actual issues can diverge from their own opinions. But given these limitations, what can we suggest as generalizations about political parties and representation in the Storting?

Our presentation of the data above makes the clear point that how parties represent voters, and how well, varies according to the issue. However, majorities of the party groups in Parliament and majorities of the same parties' voters usually end up on the same side of issues. At this most basic level, the parties do a satisfactory job of representing the voters who put them there.[2] There are occasional exceptions, noted above. More often than not, the Storting members take more extreme positions than the voters of their own parties, who tend to cluster toward the middle of the spectrum. Party activists and Storting members are usually closer together than either is to the rank-and-file voters of their respective parties. The parties at the ideological extremes—the Socialist Left and the Progress Party—display greater internal differences on issues than the other parties. While their voters do not look very different from those who vote for other parties, their Storting delegations are distinctive.

All of this suggests that the party mandate model does not provide much help in understanding political representation in Norway or other countries like it. Political parties in Norway do provide linkages between voters and governments. But these links are not always strong or concerned with contemporary issues. The process of policy representation, to say nothing of other kinds of political representation, is too complex and too continuous to be reduced to intermittent electoral mandates alone.

8

Political Groups

G roups provide important linkages between governors and those who are governed. To repeat this conventional wisdom is not to say very much. Almost any human collectivity can be called a group. Large, formal, bureaucratic organizations (the Norwegian Federation of Trade Unions, for example); informal and transitory gatherings (an audience at a ski jump); huge categories of persons sharing some characteristic (manual workers) all can be referred to as groups. And the linkages between leaders and followers that groups are said to provide can take many forms. Obviously we must limit and specify what we are talking about when writing about groups and representation.

In this chapter we will examine the literal representation of large demographic groups in the membership of the Storting. The inclusion of private group members in the official decision-making process lies at the heart of corporatist governance in legislatures as well as in executive agencies. In the next chapter we shall study the more pluralist relationships between private, nonparty groups and the Storting. In both instances, of course, we shall focus on how group politics contributes (or fails to contribute) to the policy and symbolic responsiveness of the Norwegian Storting.

The Democratization of the Storting Membership

In a famous essay Jens Arup Seip referred to the early years of Norwegian government under the Constitution of 1814 as an *embedsmannsstat,* a civil servants' state (Seip, 1963). The Storting during these years was largely staffed by civil servants, supplemented by smaller numbers of merchants and freeholding farmers. Not surprisingly most were university educated, most were late-middle-aged, and all were men (figures 8.1–8.4). This profile was largely foreordained—only males twenty-five years of age and

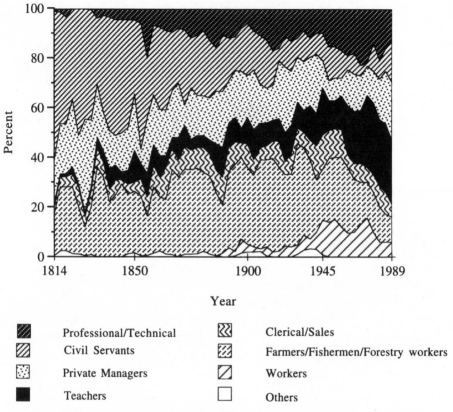

Figure 8.1 Occupations of Storting Members, by Election Period, 1814–1989.
Source: Norwegian Social Science Data Service, *Politikerarkivet* (Political archives).

older who were government officials, propertied merchants, or free-holding farmers could vote under the original Eidsvold constitution. Elections to the Storting were indirect, voters chose electors who then chose the Storting members—another mechanism favoring those already in power. Much of Norwegian political history has been devoted to describing the long, convoluted process that transformed this sharply limited form of popular government into today's mass democracy. Here we can only point out some of the more theoretically intriguing aspects of this process as illustrated by our data.

The first official steps toward opening up access to the Storting did not occur until the 1880s and '90s, when political parties were formed, parliamentary government inaugurated, and universal manhood suffrage adopted. But these portentous reforms could not have occurred if the

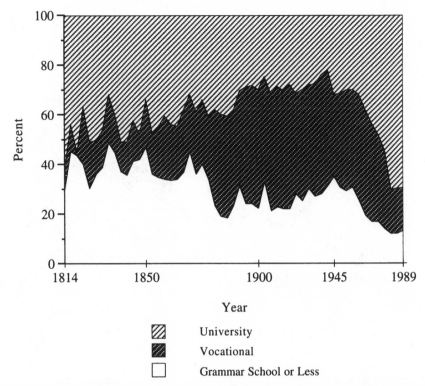

Figure 8.2 Education Levels of Storting Members, by Election Period, 1814–
1989. *Source:* Norwegian Social Science Data Service, *Politikerarkivet* (Political archives).

unreformed Storting had not responded to change in Norwegian society.
Re-examining figures 8.1–8.4, note that during the nineteenth century
the social composition of the Storting very gradually drifted towards a
more literal representation of the society as a whole. There were fewer
civil servants, more professionals and farmers. The growing popularity of
democratic ideas and the increasing conflicts between urban and rural
areas, prosperous and poor people, the right and the left were reflected,
no matter how imperfectly, in Storting debates and decisions. The Storting became somewhat representative before it became democratic.

Once conflictual, competitive politics and some degree of representation came to the Storting, further democratization was inevitable. Political parties emerged, connecting parliamentary factions to their followers
outside the chamber and making it easier for a larger and less lettered
electorate to pursue its own interest. Parliamentary government made

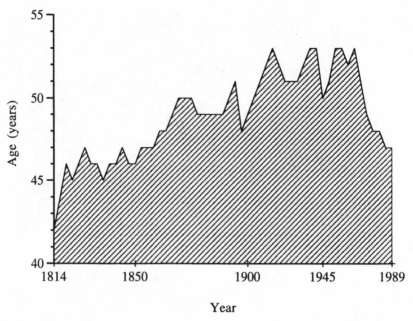

Figure 8.3 Average Age of Storting Members, by Election Period, 1814–1989. *Source:* Norwegian Social Science Data Service, *Politikerarkivet* (Political archives).

the struggle for parliamentary dominance worthwhile. The Left—and later the Labor Party—stood to gain by expanding the circle of the effectively enfranchised. In 1898, universal manhood suffrage was adopted; indirect elections were abandoned for direct election in 1905; women's suffrage was achieved in 1907 and 1913; PR was adopted in 1919. These reforms were adopted by an unreformed Storting.

But most things look inevitable in hindsight. The expansion of the suffrage and reforms of the electoral system led to a democratized Storting. But changes in response to governmental reform can be slow and partial and seem anything but inevitable to those living through them. The Labor Party was founded in 1887. It took sixteen years to elect its first member to the Storting and forty-one years to form its first government (which survived for only two weeks). Universal women's suffrage was adopted in 1913 but it wasn't until the late 1960s that more than a trace of women were elected to the Storting.

Many of these changes in the social characteristics of Stortingsmen were associated with the formation of new political parties with distinctive electoral bases. The Labor Party, with its voter support firmly rooted in the working class, provided for the first time an avenue of ascent to the

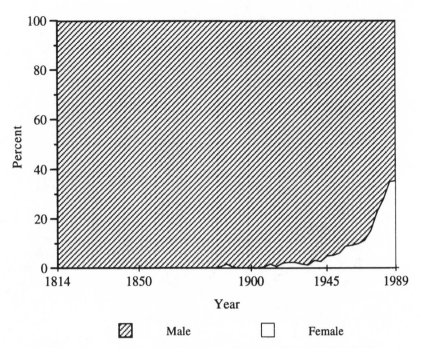

Figure 8.4 Gender of Storting Members, by Election Period, 1814–1989. *Source:* Norwegian Social Science Data Service, *Politikerarkivet* (Political archives).

Storting for manual workers. While the number of workers in the Storting has never been large—even during the heyday of the Labor Party they numbered less than one-fifth of the entire membership of the Storting—virtually all workers who have served in the Storting have been members of the Labor Party, or the Socialist Left or Communist parties (fig. 8.5). Perhaps even more important, the socialist parties have provided political opportunities to the sons and daughters of workers, which the bourgeois parties did not. Of the 455 children of manual workers who served in the Storting between 1945 and 1989, 364 (82 percent) were members of the socialist parties.

Teachers are the preponderant occupational group in all the parties founded since World War II: the Christian People's (founded in 1933, but not active nationally until 1945), the Socialist Left (founded in 1975), and the Progress Party (founded in 1973 as Anders Langes Party). The members of the new parties at the extremes of the ideological spectrum have been much the youngest members of the Storting since 1945 (fig. 8.6).

New parties are started by people who feel that they are not being

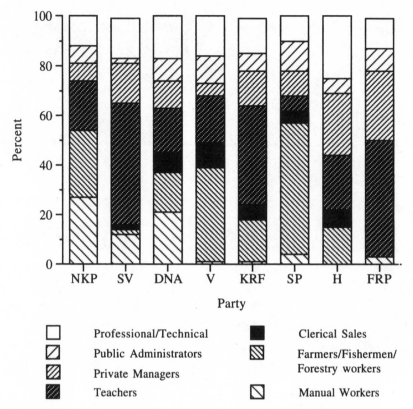

Figure 8.5 Occupations of Storting Members, by Party, 1945–1989. *Source:* Norwegian Social Science Data Service, *Politikerarkivet* (Political archives).

adequately represented by existing parties; therefore, they tend to have different social bases than the established parties. This fact is reflected in the social composition of the new parties' electoral lists and, if the parties are successful at winning seats in the Storting, eventually in their parliamentary delegations.

The pace of political change has increased noticeably since the reestablishment of peacetime politics in 1945. More teachers, professionals, and managers and fewer farmers, fishermen, foresters, and workers; younger and more highly educated members; and a rapidly increasing number of women have been elected to the Storting since World War II.

By far the most significant difference between the members of the Storting and those they represent is that the members are almost all experienced public or party officeholders (table 8.1). Between 85 percent and 92 percent of the members in every Storting session since 1945 have

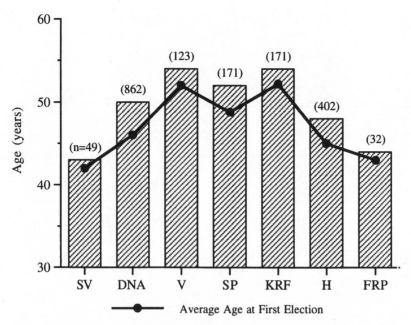

Figure 8.6   Average Age of Storting Members, by Party, 1945–1989. *Source:* Norwegian Social Science Data Service, *Politikerarkivet* (Political archives).

Table 8.1
Political Experience of Storting Members

	% of Members with Specified Experience			
	National Party Official	Fylke Councils	Party Official	Municipal Council
1945–49	37	13	56	88
1949–53	39	21	63	91
1953–57	47	23	72	92
1957–61	46	23	79	93
1961–65	45	21	73	92
1965–69	45	25	72	90
1969–73	41	29	67	89
1973–77	45	34	70	90
1977–81	36	38	77	87
1981–85	26	36	74	85
1985–89	23	35	70	87
1989–93	27	45	74	87

served as members of municipal councils, and between 56 percent and 79 percent have served as party officials. In recent years from a quarter to a half have served in fylke councils and more than a quarter in national party leadership positions. There is little difference between the parties on this matter. Members of the Storting without regard to party are atypical Norwegians in the extent of their political activity and achievement. Combine this with the fact that today's members have spent many more years in schools and universities than their predecessors and are elected to the Storting earlier in life, and you have today a legislature of mostly career politicians.

The Feminization of the Storting

While the democratization of the Storting was a prolonged process, the feminization of Norway's national Parliament came on with a rush.[1] After a slow start, women achieved near parity in parliamentary representation with men in the 1970s and '80s. The Storting became a world leader in gender equality. This process deserves special treatment.[2]

The number of women serving in the Storting never exceeded 10 percent from 1921, when the first woman was elected, until the 1970s, when the number of women in the Storting suddenly started to skyrocket (see fig. 8.4). In 1973, twenty-four women (15.5 percent of the membership) were elected; in 1977, thirty-seven (24 percent); in 1981, forty (26 percent); in 1985, fifty-four (34 percent); in 1989, fifty-nine (36 percent). While the Socialist Left and the Labor Party led the way—51 percent of the Labor and 41 percent of the Socialist Left members were women by 1989—all the other parties, except the Progress Party, quickly followed their lead with delegations more than a quarter female. Gro Harlem Brundtland became Norway's first woman prime minister in 1981, and no cabinet since then has failed to represent women heavily. Most of the political parties have selected women as national leaders for at least a portion of the years since 1980.

What accounts for this abrupt departure from the initial pattern of glacial gains for gender equality? Why did this occur in Norway while the old pattern still prevails in many other advanced democracies?

Two easy explanations can be largely dismissed from the start. While Norwegian culture stresses the values of equality and community, this culture did not drastically reduce the resistance to the feminization of politics that has occurred. Equality of the sexes—socially and economically—has a long way to go in Norway (Haavio-Mannila, 1981; Skard and

Haavio-Mannila, 1984). Gender stereotyping of political candidates is still widespread (Matland, 1994). Second, a "great person" explanation is unconvincing. Gro Harlem Brundtland is unquestionably Norway's most popular and effective political leader in recent decades. Her rapid and unexpected rise to the leadership of the country's largest party and the prime ministership is testimony to her imposing skill, energy and good luck (a quality Machiavelli recommended to all rulers). As prime minister, she was able to dramatize and symbolize gender issues in ways that speeded up the process of change. But occasional extraordinary women have become prime ministers—Margaret Thatcher, Golda Meier, Indira Ghandi—without appreciably altering the male domination of the politics of their country. More than a single great woman is required to bring about changes of this magnitude.

Our explanation of the feminization of the Storting stresses four political and institutional factors.

1. First of all, a sizable pool of potential parliamentary candidates had to exist before many women could be elected to the Storting. This was the slow part of the process. Many women had to break from traditional gender roles in the home and family and gain advanced education, experience in the workplace, leadership roles in private organizations and local politics, and the self-confidence needed to succeed in the confrontational political world (Valen, 1989). Given the exceptionally high value placed upon prior political experience for Storting nominations, experience at the local level was especially important in the creation of this pool of eligibles. While the rate at which women were elected to local office was about the same as the rate at which women were elected to the Storting, the absolute numbers of women with local elective experience grew substantially in the 1950s and '60s (Heidar, 1983: 301, table 10.3). These numbers do not include women serving in provincial councils or in local party offices.

Year	No. of Women Elected to City Councils
1951	890
1955	1,056
1959	978
1963	904
1967	1,291
1971	1,985
1975	2,087
1979	3,140

2. A second precondition for the feminization of the Storting was some degree of political mobilization of Norwegian women. At a minimum this involved women voting at approximately the same rate as men, a situation that was achieved well before the 1960s. Feminism came to Norway in the 1960s and the '70s, inspired in part by the movement in the United States, and created a politically mobilized leadership group of women.

In 1971, taking advantage of election laws that permitted voters to alter electoral lists in local elections, women elected majorities to the city councils of three municipalities—Asker, Oslo and Trondheim—and more than 40 percent of the seats in six other cities. This created quite an uproar—and the electoral laws were quickly changed to make it more difficult to employ the strategy again. But the incident demonstrated that women could be mobilized to support other women in elections in Norway with striking results. Ten years later, Mrs. Brundtland's choice as leader of the Labor Party and hence prime minister was aided and abetted by a massive, nationwide grass-roots campaign—letters, telegrams, telephone calls—organized in only a few days and focused on the party committee that was to make the choice (and that initially favored an established male politician).[3] There were loud complaints about this "un-Norwegian" way of doing things and gloomy references to the Americanization of Norwegian politics. But Brundtland won, and remained the leader of the country's largest party until she stepped down in 1996.

3. The third condition leading to the rapid increase in women Storting members in the 1960s and '70s was the country's proportional representation electoral system. Such electoral arrangements are statistically associated with relatively large numbers of women in elective office (Rule, 1987). The reason for this is clear. In a PR-list system as in Norway, each electoral district is represented by several legislators—from four to sixteen in the Norwegian case. The political parties nominate ranked lists of candidates for the seats in each of the districts and voters vote for one of the party's lists. It is much easier for a woman politician to gain a place on a party list of candidates than for her to become the party's sole candidate in a single-member district system. Similarly, it is easier for voters unaccustomed to female politicians to vote for a slate of candidates that contains one or more women than to vote for a woman over a man in a zero-sum, single-member district contest.

This is illustrated by the fact that during the period of rapid transformation from a Parliament with a few token women members to one in which women were represented at near parity, women most often won

Table 8.2

Female Representation in Storting

Year	% of Storting Female	Correlation between District Size and % Female	Correlation between District Party Delegation Size and % Female
1953	4.7	−0.5	.34**
1957	6.7	.21	.45**
1961	8.7	.28	.52**
1965	8.0	.43*	.32**
1969	9.3	.36	.38**
1973	15.5	.15	.25*
1977	23.9	.21	.20
1981	25.8	−.04	.24*
1985	34.4	.02	.15
1989	35.8	.30	.20

Source: Matland (1993), 741, table 1.

$*p \leq .05$, $**p \leq .01$.

seats in the larger delegations (Matland, 1993). In table 8.2, the correlations between the size of the provincial delegation and the size of party delegation and the percentage of women elected to the Storting between 1953 and 1989 are presented. The correlation between the size of the provincial delegation and the percentage of women in that delegation is positive but not statistically significant. The correlation with party delegation size, however, is much larger and statistically significant during the take-off period. As the number of women in the Storting increased, and the bourgeois parties joined the bandwagon in nominating more and more women, the correlation between district party delegation size and the percentage of women elected seems to decline as women's opportunities improve. Even so, women tend to do better in delegations with an even number of seats (a 50-50 split is easy) than where a party wins an odd number of seats (the extra seat always goes to a male) (Matland, 1995).

4. A final condition that contributed to the rapid feminization of the Parliament is the making of party nominations by provincial party conventions. These ad hoc assemblies of local party leaders are interested in preserving party unity and winning the next election. Usually these twin desires suggest a balanced ticket representing the various factions within the local party. Like the American party conventions, after which they were modeled, members of the fylke conventions are elected at sparsely

attended local meetings of partisans. Usually this results in a small group of longtime party activists controlling the local meetings and thus the provincial conventions. But low turnout and mass acquiescence can—and sometimes do—disappear. The regulars show up at the local party meeting to be greeted by many new faces, mobilized into action by some new action, group, or issue, clutching their newly paid-up party membership cards. This happens from time to time in the United States (i.e., presidential nominations in the Democratic Party during the Vietnam War). It happened in Norway, and the issue was female representation. This does not have to occur too many times before the (largely male) established local politicians who have traditionally controlled candidate access to party lists decide to go along with the tide rather than be overwhelmed. Shared power is better than none at all. Finally, at the national level, the party conventions—first the parties of the left, next the center, and then the right—adopted gender quotas for Storting nominations. The Storting was feminized.

Symbolic and Policy Representation

At the symbolic level, the members of the Storting represent the absent others better than most other national legislatures do (Matthews, 1954; Putnam, 1976). It may be safe to assume that this adds to the legitimacy of the institution and its decisions. But does this symbolic representation lead to policy representation as well? It would be unwise to assume an answer to this question.

Do Social Characteristics Matter?

If the social and economic characteristics of members of a legislature are unrelated to how the members vote on issues, then it is hard to see how those characteristics can affect policy representation. Thus an obvious first step in exploring the relationship between symbolic and policy representation is to check out this possibility. Unfortunately, this proves to be more difficult than it at first appears. Most votes in the Storting are not recorded for individual members, so we must analyze the members' responses to a battery of issue questions we asked them instead of their official votes. And most of the rich detail we have about the members' backgrounds must be ignored in order to have enough cases to permit statistical analysis. Constraints of this sort are common in empirical research, but still need to be kept in mind as we proceed.

In table 8.3, the 1985 policy views of members of the Storting belonging to different groups are compared on eighteen issues. Each member's opinion on each issue was assigned a score ranging from 1 (complete agreement with the statement in the questionnaire) to 5 (complete disagreement). The scores were averaged for each group, and the difference in the means between groups is presented in the table, along with the level of statistical significance of the differences. If the level of statistical significance is less than .05, the difference in the means has been omitted in order to facilitate comprehension of the table.

It is immediately apparent that members of the Storting with different social backgrounds have decidedly different policy views. On the eighteen policy issues in our questionnaire, men and women in the Storting differ at a statistically significant level on thirteen. In all thirteen cases, the women as a group were to the left of the men. The largest differences between the sexes were on the issues of sexual equality, environmental protection, level of public expenditure, and support for nursery schools. The occupations of members of the Storting were almost as divisive as gender—"high" and "low" occupation groups have statistically significant differences in the mean scores on eleven of the eighteen issues. These large differences were mainly found on economic issues—taxes, government expenditure levels, home loans, and so on—but there were large differences on foreign and defense policy as well. No other personal characteristic of the members is as strongly associated with their policy views as gender and occupation. But there were statistically significant differences in mean scores between university-educated members and those with less formal education on six issues, between those over and under forty years of age on five; between those whose fathers had higher or lower occupations on five, between urban and rural dwellers on four, and between those born in urban or rural areas on two. The social and economic backgrounds of members are thus related to their policy commitments, and the magnitude of those differences is large. Symbolic representation within the Storting may contribute to policy representation for some groups on some issues.

But what happens to those relationships between the members' personal backgrounds and their policy preferences when we look at them for the political parties separately? The Storting parties are highly disciplined, presenting a united front to the rest of the world most of the time.

Table 8.3

Difference in Mean Scale Scores on Policy Issues by Demographic Groups within Storting, 1985

	Gender Male/Female	Occupation Lower/Higher	Education Univ./No Univ.	Age ≤ 40/> 40	Father's Occupation Lower/Higher	Residence Urban/Rural	Birthplace Urban/Rural
Economic policies							
Lower taxes	−0.48**	+0.92**	−0.59**		−0.50*	−0.48*	−0.67**
Lower home loan interest		+0.45**	+0.28*		−0.29*		
Economic aid to periphery						+0.37*	+0.38*
Reduce state regulation					+0.44*		
Stop growth of public expense	−0.73***	+0.71***		+0.57*			
Expand public sector to reduce unemployment	+0.46*	−0.67**	+0.61**		−0.46*		
Subsidize urban economy	+0.35*					−0.31*	
Foreign and defense policies							
Stronger national defense	+0.64**	+0.55***		+0.42*			
Forbid atomic weapons	+0.57*	−1.11***	+0.55*		−0.70**		
More aid to developing countries						+0.40*	

Welfare policies					
More social equalization	+0.30*	−0.50***	−0.32*		−0.42**
Forbid private hospitals		−0.80**	+0.60*		
More nursery schools	+0.68***	−0.40*		−0.43*	
Non-economic issues					
More sexual equality	+0.62***				
Strengthen Christian morality	−0.49**				
Environmental protection	+0.37***	−0.24*		+0.72**	
Tighten admission of immigrants	−0.53**				
Abolish grading in secondary schools	+0.59**	−0.75***		−0.62*	

Notes: Differences in means are figured (first listed group) − (second listed group); i.e., (male mean) − (female mean), etc.

Scale scores vary from 1.0 (completely in favor) to 5.0 (completely opposed).

Differences in means omitted if not statistically significant at .05 or better.

$*p \leq .05$, $**p \leq .01$, $***p \leq .001$.

Most opportunities for parliamentarians to advance their personal views and agendas exist within their respective parties. Thus, it seems important to repeat the above analysis within the parties. To do so, we must compromise further by collapsing the parties into two blocs—the socialist parties and the bourgeois parties—in order to have enough cases for analysis. The results are presented in tables 8.4 and 8.5.

The first thing to note is that the gender differences between members of the Storting remain even after controlling for party bloc. This is especially the case among socialists, where the women, on average, were more left wing than the men at statistically significant levels on eleven different issues. The gender gap among the nonsocialists was smaller and confined to noneconomic issues such as sexual equality and environmental protection, but still in the same direction. Second, the strong correlation between the members' occupations (including the occupations of their fathers) and their policy preferences disappears when examined within the two blocs. Class-based economic conflict has so dominated Norwegian party politics in modern times that occupational conflict and party conflict have become nearly indistinguishable. Differences in age and education levels show up on a few issues among the socialists—national defense, Christian morality, and grading policy in the schools—but don't seem to matter on other issues or among the nonsocialists. Finally, members of the Storting with urban and rural backgrounds differ on policy issues about as often within party blocs as for the chamber as a whole. This is especially true within the nonsocialist bloc.[4] These differences seem to be partly economic; the urban and rural members tend to line up on opposite sides of proposals allocating resources to the city or to the rural periphery and also on the newer noneconomic issues such as environmental politics and immigration. The conclusion is inescapable: the social characteristics of members do matter.

Members vs. Voters

Do these group differences within the Storting reflect group differences outside? For example, when men and women within the Parliament disagree, does this represent a similar disagreement between men and women in the electorate? Our data suggest a complex answer to this question.

In figure 8.7 we examine the policy preferences of members of the Storting and the electorate on five different issues in 1985. Given the great

Table 8.4

Difference in Mean Scale Scores on Policy Issues of Socialists, 1985, by Demographic Groups

	Gender Male/Female	Occupation Lower/Higher	Education Univ./No Univ.	Age ≤ 40/> 40	Father's Occupation Lower/Higher	Residence Urban/Rural	Birthplace Urban/Rural
Economic policies							
Lower taxes	– .65**						
Lower home loan interest			+0.32*				
Economic aid to periphery							
Reduce state regulation							
Stop growth of public expense	– .68**						
Expand public sector to reduce unemployment	+ .60*					– .57**	
Subsidize urban economy							
Foreign and defense policies							
Stronger national defense			+ .44*				
Forbid atomic weapons	+ .61**						

continued

Table 8.4
continued

	Gender Male/Female	Occupation Lower/Higher	Education Univ./No Univ.	Age ≤ 40/> 40	Father's Occupation Lower/Higher	Residence Urban/Rural	Birthplace Urban/Rural
More aid to developing countries	+.63*						
Welfare policies							
More social equalization	+.46***					−.27*	−.25*
Forbid private hospitals							
More nursery schools	+.63***						−.45**
Non-economic issues							
More sexual equality	+.59**		−.61*				
Strengthen Christian morality				+.84**			
Environmental protection	+.38*						
Tighten admission of immigrants	−.71**						
Abolish grading in secondary schools	+.57**						

Notes: See table 8.3.

$*p \leq .05$, $**p \leq .01$, $***p \leq .001$.

Table 8.5

Difference in Mean Scale Scores on Policy Issues of Non-Socialists, 1985, by Demographic Groups

	Gender Male/Female	Occupation Lower/Higher	Education Univ./No Univ.	Age ≤ 40/> 40	Father's Occupation Lower/Higher	Residence Urban/Rural	Birthplace Urban/Rural
Economic policies							
Lower taxes							
Lower home loan interest							
Economic aid to periphery							− .73**
Reduce state regulation							
Stop growth of public expense							+ .67**
Expand public sector to reduce unemployment							
Subsidize urban economy							
Foreign and defense policies							
Stronger national defense			− .56*				
Forbid atomic weapons						+ .57*	+ .69*
More aid to developing countries		− .66*					+ .53*

continued

Table 8.5
continued

	Gender Male/Female	Occupation Lower/Higher	Education Univ./No Univ.	Age ≤ 40/> 40	Father's Occupation Lower/Higher	Residence Urban/Rural	Birthplace Urban/Rural
Welfare policies							
More social equalization							
Forbid private hospitals							
More nursery schools							
Non-economic issues							
More sexual equality							
Strengthen Christian morality							
Environmental protection	+.50*						
Tighten admission of immigrants	−.49*						.26**
Abolish grading in secondary schools	+.34*				−.39*	−.49*	.50***

Notes: See table 8.3.

$*p \leq .05$, $**p \leq .01$, $***p \leq .001$.

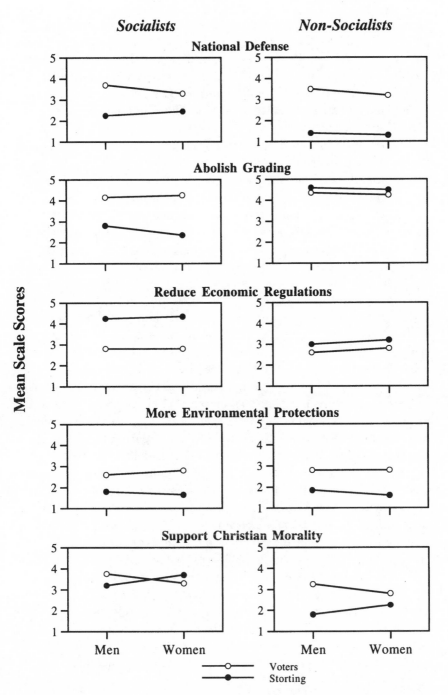

Figure 8.7 Gender and Policy Preferences of Storting Members and Voters, 1985

importance of party, we further divide both the voters and the Storting members into party blocs—socialist and nonsocialist. Within each of the five issues and two blocs, we present the mean scale scores on issues of the members and voters by gender. This permits us to examine the extent of policy agreement between members and voters with similar characteristics and to compare the relative importance of this agreement to the impact of party and issues.

The first and probably the most important conclusion that emerges is that the policy preferences of Storting members often diverge from the preferences of voters who share the same party bloc and gender. The extent of this divergence varies by issue and party. The members of the Storting, for example, are much more inclined to support a strong national defense than voters of the same gender and party bloc. This is especially true within the bourgeois parties and among men, but it is sizable in both party groups and genders. The next issue—the proposal to abolish grading in the secondary schools—is supported by left-wing leaders of Labor and the Socialist Left, especially women, and vehemently opposed by everyone else, including the rank and file of their own party bloc. The extent of government regulation of the economy is an issue lying at the center of the conflict between socialists and nonsocialists for generations. Even so, the socialists in the Storting are much more in favor of government regulation of the economy than socialist voters, while the nonsocialists tend to agree in opposition. Gender seems unimportant on this issue. Environmental protection, however, is favored by members of the Storting in both blocs far more than voters in their respective blocs. Women Storting members are especially pro-environment. On the last issue—taking steps to strengthen Christian faith and morality—Storting members tend to be more favorable than comparable voters. An important exception to this tendency are the socialist women, who again take a more left-wing position than socialist women voters.

In figure 8.8 we compare the policy preferences of Storting members and voters by level of occupation. A similar picture emerges of the relative importance of party bloc, Storting membership, and personal background in shaping policy preferences. Occupation does seem to make some difference in most of the five issues we examine, but the differences are usually much smaller than the differences between party blocs and between members of the Storting and voters with similar demographic characteristics. This seems to be the case no matter what demographic groups we compare.

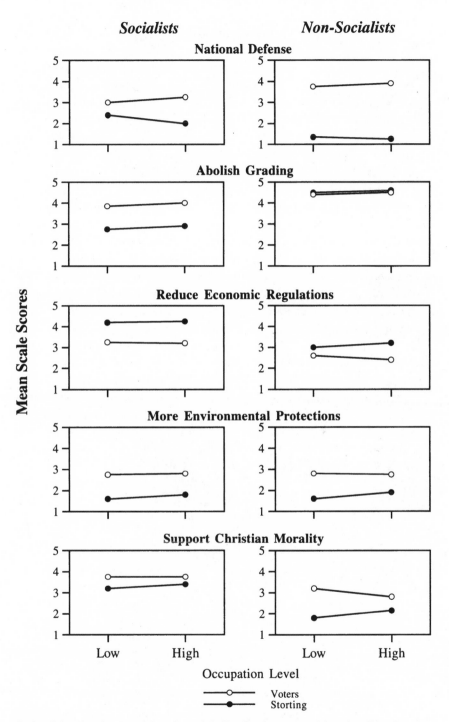

Figure 8.8 Occupational Levels and Policy Preferences of Storting Members and Voters, 1985

Conclusions

In this chapter we have examined the inclusion and exclusion of demographic groups within the Storting—a form of symbolic representation. We have described how the social composition of the Storting has changed since 1814 in response to changes in Norwegian society and the rules of the political game. We have focused on the process of change with special attention given to the most recent of these changes, the dramatic feminization of the Storting in the 1970s and '80s.

Today, members of the Storting come in a variety of sizes and shapes, socially and economically speaking. They are neither a perfect representation of the diversity of Norwegian society nor a group drawn exclusively from its more prominent and privileged circles. While better-off Norwegians are over-represented, this distortion is not as large as in most other countries. The most important way the Storting differs from the absent others is that the members are almost all experienced local government and party officeholders and, increasingly, are career politicians who have limited experience at doing anything else.

Finally, we examined the relationship between the members' social characteristics and their policy preferences. These relationships are numerous and strong, but mostly run parallel with party lines rather than cutting across them. Members of different social groups in the Storting do not automatically agree with the members of the same groups outside the legislature—sometimes they do, sometimes they don't, depending upon the issue. Party and membership in the Storting itself seem to be more important influences on policy preferences than other group affiliations.

9

The Storting:
Organization and Processes

The person in the street pays attention to the Storting mostly around election time. But representation is a continuous process. While elections shape that process, what happens in a legislature *between* elections is ultimately what matters. In this chapter we shall look at the Storting between elections and some ways in which its organization and processes affect representation. Specifically, we shall describe and analyze the different ways members of the Storting define who or what they represent. Then we will move on to look at patterns of work in the Storting, especially how members allocate their time and energy, and some of the implications of these patterns.

The standing committees of the Storting are where most of the chambers' work is done. Given the number and complexity of the issues the Storting faces, a division of labor is essential. Yet strong, autonomous committees pose potential principal-agent problems. The ways the Storting seeks to control its own committees is discussed, with comparisons to another legislature with strong committees, the U.S. Congress. Finally, we shall look at the extensive contacts and communications members have with private groups and associations and estimate how much difference such contacts make for the Storting as a representative institution.

Who or What to Represent?

Electoral districts for the Storting are large, represented by several members from several political parties. Realistically, no member can represent the entire district; the member must define who or what to represent. This inescapable fact of parliamentary life presents opportunities and risks. Members do not make this decision all at once, for all time. Rather, who and what a member represents emerges from decisions on other more limited and immediate questions.

Member choices about who or what to represent are sharply constrained. No one gets elected to the Storting who is not a "good party person," as defined by the local party activists who put together party lists. The allocation of committee assignments and other desirable things within the Storting are largely controlled by the leadership of the parliamentary party groups. In the long run, the political future of Storting members depends upon the approval of these and other party leadership cadres in Oslo and back home. Thus, it is not surprising that most members of the Storting say that they represent their party. When asked, in 1985, "Do you consider yourself, first and foremost, as a spokesperson for your party or your district?," 60 percent of the members said their party, 5 percent said their district, and 35 percent said both.[1]

It is not clear, however, what representing one's party means. Does the member represent party leaders, members, or party voters? Is the party viewed as the local or national party—or the party in the legislature? When the party is not of one mind, what then? Thus we also asked the members (at a different point in the interview) whether they were spokespersons for "specific interests, ideas, and demands within the scope of the party." More than 70 percent answered "yes." This proportion was about the same for all parties.[2] Those answering "yes" were then asked which "interests, ideas, or demands" they spoke for. We received the responses presented in table 9.1. Well over half of the members asked said they spoke for some kind of a group within the party—women, the major economic groups in the society, children and young people. About one-third said they represented their district, or some locality within their district, and about a quarter reported that they represented an idea or policy position. Clearly, "good party men and women" can and do see themselves as representing different things.

This tendency is encouraged by the fact that members of the Storting have run for office as part of a team. These teams are put together by local party leaders inclined to create candidate slates representative of the various ideas and interests in the locality. This strategy reduces conflict within the local party and probably increases the electability of the party's team. It also provides new members with a clear indication of why they were placed on the list. When asked why they were first nominated, more than 80 percent of all members answered in representational terms: they represented a geographical area within the district (26 percent), they represented women (17 percent); they represented their age group (19 percent), occupation (12 percent), or union (8 percent). Political expe-

Table 9.1
Interests, Ideas, or Demands That Members are Spokespersons for (%)

	Members by Party				All Members	N
	DNA	SP	KrF	H		
Districts and localities	32	54.5	61	24	32	48
Groups	72	45	30	42	55.5	80
Women	22.5	9	15	16	18	26
Agriculture, Forestry, Fishing	14	27	—	7	11	16
Industry	10	19	—	12	10	14
Trade unions	17	—	—	—	9	13
Youth/children	8.5	—	15	7	7.5	11
Ideology/policies	17.5	27	47	35	27.5	40
Environmental policy	8.5	18	—	9	9	13
Social/health policy	4	9	8	7	6	9
Education policy	1	—	23	7	55	8
Ideology	3	—	8	7	4	6
Culture policy	1	—	8	5	3	4

Notes: Interests mentioned three or fewer times omitted. Breakdowns for the Socialist Left and Progress parties omitted because of small numbers. SV and FrP responses are included in the percentages for all members.

rience was cited as a major reason for their initial nomination, too. Thirty-three percent mentioned experience as a factor, 28 percent mentioned prior political activity, and 8 percent party officeholding. These reasons for being nominated no doubt affect members' decisions about who or what to represent.

But not all members say they represent their party. What about the members who say they primarily represent their districts or who say they represent their party and district equally? They are in the minority, but it is a sizable minority; 40 percent of the membership say they are more district-oriented than the others.

A close look reveals differences between Storting members who are party-oriented and those who are district-oriented. While both types of legislators can be found throughout the country, those from the more isolated and rural parts of Norway—the Southwest and the North—are much more likely to be district-oriented than the others (table 9.2). Those from the Southeast and the cities and suburbs are mostly party-oriented members. There is also a class difference between the groups—

Table 9.2

Characteristics and Representational Orientation of Members (%)

	Party-oriented	District-oriented	N
Region			
Oslo fjord	75	25	40
Eastern interior	50	50	14
South	60	40	10
West	51	49	35
Trøndelag	71	29	14
North	35	65	20
Urban/rural residence			
Oslo	86	14	14
Other cities	60	40	48
Suburbs	87	13	8
Rural areas	46	54	65
Occupational class			
High functionary	66	34	59
Middle functionary	59	41	39
Low functionary	37	63	8
Primary sector worker	33	67	9
Industrial worker	17	83	6
Seniority: Length of Service			
1 or 2 terms	51	49	55
3 or 4 terms	61	39	61
5+ terms	75	25	16

those with high-status jobs tend to be party-oriented members, and lower-status workers are overwhelmingly district-oriented.

How a member of the Storting defines his or her representational roles is not a constant. New members may be especially prone to focus on their district and its needs; after all, they know their constituency well or they probably would not be there. But service in the Storting is an educational experience. Members are exposed to many new and different ideas and perspectives and service on committees can develop new areas of expertise. As their tenures lengthen, they become better known, their names rise toward the top of their electoral lists, they are more politically secure. They become national politicians. Gudmund Hernes found this happening for many members more than twenty years ago (1971). Our data are consistent with that finding. In the 1985–89 session, at least, the most senior members were much more likely to be party-oriented than the relative newcomers (table 9.2).

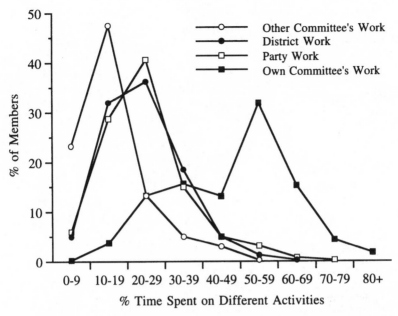

Figure 9.1 Allocation of Time by Storting Members, 1985–1989

Work: The Allocation of Time and Energy

One way of comprehending what a legislature does is to look at how its members spend their time. In figure 9.1, we present the overall picture for the members serving in the 1985–89 session of the Storting. It displays the percentage of their time in the Storting that members devote to their committee work, to their district duties and party responsibilities, and to other matters outside the jurisdiction of their own committee.

Committee Work

Clearly the standing committees are the most important work groups in the Storting; a large majority of the members spent most of their time and energy within the single standing committee upon which they serve. The twelve standing committees have jurisdiction roughly corresponding to that of the executive departments and must pass on all legislative and budgetary proposals received from the government before they are considered in plenary sessions. Committees meet behind closed doors, and their decisions, especially if they are unanimous, are seldom overturned at later, more public stages of the legislative process. The Storting's

Table 9.3
Members' Committee Preferences, 1985 (%)

Committee	1 of 3 Committees R Would Most Like to Be Member Of	1 of 3 Committees R Would Least Like to Be Member Of
Industry	47	2
Finance	46	12.5
Local Government	45	3
Communications	36	1
Foreign Affairs	34	8
Social Affairs	25	12.5
Education	22	10
Defense	14.5	28
Fisheries	9	58
Judiciary	8	44
Agriculture	6	55
Administration	4	56

committees are not as powerful or autonomous as those in the United States Congress; they initiate no legislation, hold no public hearings calculated to sway public opinion, and co-exist with highly disciplined parliamentary parties. But they are where most of the action is.

The committees differ in their attractiveness to members. Some committees are very popular—almost half of all the members would like to serve on Industry or Finance or Local Government (table 9.3). At the same time, four other committees—Fisheries, Judiciary, Agriculture, and Administration—are preferred by fewer than one out of every ten members. There is thus a definite pecking order among the committees and a large imbalance between the supply and demand of "good" committee assignments. This, of course, makes the allocation of committee seats more difficult than it would be if committee preferences were distributed more randomly. It also means that some committees are made up of members who want to be on the committee while other committees consist primarily of draftees. The implications of these differences will be developed below.

On the whole, the most desirable committees take the most time. Finance, which presides over the budget, and Industry, which is involved with major economic issues, are the hardest working committees in the Storting. But some highly desirable committee assignments—Foreign Affairs and the politically potent Local Government Committee—are much less demanding of members' time and energy.

Members of the Storting, as legislators in other countries (Fenno, 1973), probably want to serve on committees that can help them achieve their goals. In order to explore this idea, we asked the Storting members to rank the committees on the basis of five criteria: In which committee can you do the most for your district? For your party's program? For your own influence? Which committees have the most prestige? Which deal with the most important matters for the country? The responses are summarized in table 9.4. The benefits of service differ according to committee. The Local Government, Industry and Communications committees are seen to be the ones from which members can do the most for their districts. The Finance Committee—the most prestigious and important of the standing committees—comes in a poor fourth on this dimension. Almost no one believed that service on Defense, Administration, Judiciary, or Foreign Affairs helped members serve their districts. When it comes to contributing to the members' party, Finance is the overwhelming choice—89 percent chose it as a committee where members can most help their party. Other high choices are Local Government, Industry, and Education. There is less agreement about which committees most enhance the members' influence, but Local Government and Finance top the list, followed by Social Affairs, Industry, Education, and Communications.

Prestige and importance are still different matters. Finance is almost everybody's first choice in both prestige and importance. Foreign Affairs, which ranked low on the earlier dimensions, is almost everybody's second choice in prestige (84 percent) and importance (58 percent). Industry ranks third in prestige (72 percent), after which there is a huge gap before the fourth choice, Local Government (13 percent), a committee with more political importance than prestige.

Thus different committees are believed to contribute to different members' objectives. No doubt there are other goals beyond the five we have examined here. But what is the relative importance of these five goals for the Storting as a whole? We correlated the members' list of committee preferences (table 9.3) with the list of the committees on the five dimensions we studied (table 9.4). The result are presented in table 9.5. Influence turns out to be what the average member wants more than anything from his or her committee assignment. An enhanced capacity to service the district is a close second; prestige, third; an opportunity to contribute to the party, fourth; and an opportunity to work on important matters, last.

Table 9.4

Members' Evaluations of Committee Assignments, 1985 (% of Members Including Committee in Top 3 Committees, by Dimension)

Would Do Most for District	Would Do Most for Party	Would Do Most for Members' Influence	Has the Most Prestige	Deals with Most Important Matters
Local Government (71)	Finance (89)	Local Government (47.5)	Finance (95)	Finance (99)
Industry (55)	Local Government (45)	Finance (40)	Foreign Affairs (84)	Foreign Affairs (58)
Communications (54)	Industry (41)	Social Affairs (33)	Industry (72)	Industry (43)
Finance (37)	Education (21)	Industry (32)	Local Government (13)	Social Affairs (30)
Education (23)	Defense (7)	Education (29.5)	Communications (12)	Local Government (27)
Social Affairs (21)	Communications (7)	Communications (29)	Social Affairs (8)	Defense (21)
Fisheries (16)	Fisheries (7)	Fisheries (19)	Defense (6)	Education (14)
Agriculture (15)	Agriculture (6)	Agriculture (18)	Education (5)	Communications (6)
Defense (3)	Social Affairs (2)	Foreign Affairs (14)	Agriculture (1)	Agriculture (1)
Administration (1)	Foreign Affairs (2)	Administration (13)	Administration (0)	Fisheries (1)
Judiciary (1)	Administration (2)	Judiciary (11.5)	Judiciary (0)	Administration (1)
Foreign Affairs (1)	Judiciary (0)	Defense (10)	Fisheries (0)	Judiciary (0)

Table 9.5

Correlation between Members' Committee Preferences
and Perceived Benefits of Service

Perceived Benefit of Service in Committee	r
Would lead to most influence in Storting	+.80
Would do most for members' district	+.78
Has the most prestige	+.72
Would do most for the party	+.70
Deals with most important problems	+.54

District Work

Most members of the Storting in 1985–89 spent about 20 percent of their time on district work. This covers quite a variety of activities.

Visits to the district are frequent. A little more than 10 percent of the members—all from Oslo and surrounding areas—commute to the Storting on a daily basis. More than half of the members spent at least ten days a month in their district, while a third spent less. Commuters aside, geography does not seem to affect the amount of time members spend back home. Those from northern and western Norway spent about the same amount of time at home as those who live closer to Oslo.

Members of the Storting are in frequent contact with party and government officials at the municipal and provincial levels, mostly those in their own province (table 9.6). More than half say they are in touch at least once a week with the local political party. Slightly fewer than half report contact with municipal government officials at that same rate. Another 40 percent report at least monthly contacts. Communication with provincial officials is somewhat less frequent. Contacts with local officials outside their own provinces are still more infrequent.

Finally, members actively promote the interests of their districts while on the job in Oslo. About 40 percent say they often take initiative to promote their districts' interests in their own committees, another 40 percent take initiative in other committees, 30 percent in their party's group, and more than 50 percent in the departments (table 9.7). Thus district work consists of a number of different activities.

The priority given to district activities seems to diminish among members beginning at about their fifth term. The amount of time senior members give to committee work also seems to decline at about the same time.

Table 9.6
Members' Frequency of Contact with Subnational Government and Party Officials (%)

	Daily	Weekly	Monthly	Rarely	Never	Total
City officials, own province	6	41	44	8	1	100
Provincial officials, own province	1	29	46.5	22.5	1	100
City officials, other provinces	0	4	24	59	12	100
Provincial officials, other provinces	0	4	21	60	15	100
Employees in central party office	12	47	26	14	0	100

Table 9.7
Members: Do You Often Take Initiative to Promote Interest of District? (% Yes)

	Very Often	Rather Often	Sometimes	Rather Seldom	Never	Total
In your committee	15	24	46	11	4	100
In other committees' fields	7	34	48	11	0	100
In party groups	6	26	53	15	1	100
In the departments	17	35	39	7	1.5	100

The work time of the most senior members is devoted primarily to party leadership and to coordinating policies across committee lines.

Party Work

Average members of the Storting during the 1985–89 session spent about 20 percent of their time working in their party group. These caucuses meet regularly and often to thrash out the party position on measures, to develop common strategies on contested matters, to allocate rewards and responsibilities within the parliamentary party. These activities are crucially important to members; a good reputation within the party group is a necessary if not sufficient condition for a career leading to national prominence.

The legislative parties are far more important than these figures imply. Members are representatives of and spokespersons for their parties within their committees, in their dealings with their constituencies, and in just about everything else they do. This of course does not show up when the allocation of time between different activities is examined.

Work outside One's Own Committee

The committee system forces most Storting members to devote the lion's share of their time and energy to the set of issues handled by their own standing committee. But while committee power and autonomy are essential, they are not absolute. Almost all members of the Storting have ideas and represent interests that fall outside their committee's jurisdiction. This is especially true for members from the smaller parties that do not have formal representation on all the committees. The government and the political parties have elaborate policy programs that require coordinated action from many committees. Thus members of the Storting spend some of their time and energy—about 10–15 percent on the average—on legislative and budgetary matters outside the walls of their committee room.

Probably the most common form of this activity is contacting members of other committees in an effort to promote the interests of the member's district—40 percent of the members report doing this often (see table 9.6). Conversations with colleagues over coffee in the lunchroom, debates within the party group over how the party delegation in other committees should behave, and other informal and private methods of persuasion are the norm. Since all members want something from others from time to time, a spirit of reciprocity can pervade these transactions. Those who serve on committees from which everyone wants something— Finance, Communications, Local Government—can develop considerable power within the Storting as a consequence (cf. Hernes, 1971).

The members who spent the most time at this sort of work are the leaders of the Storting's political parties. Party officers report that they spend twice as much of their time on the work of committees other than their own than do rank-and-file members. The amount of time spent on other committees' problems more than doubles from the most junior to the most senior members. Thus the focus of attention of members broadens as they accumulate experience, prominence, and party leadership positions. The amount of time they spend on committee and district work declines as they devote themselves more to party leadership.

Standing Committees, Principal-Agent Problems, and Representation

Standing committees perform important functions in contemporary legislatures. They make it possible through a division of labor for a large group of politicians to process the growing number of complex issues that confront modern governments. They also ensure some measure of expertise in legislative decision-making. Committee members become more competent in dealing with their issues than the other members; thus the most knowledgeable members tend to have the most influence on legislative outcomes.

But standing committees pose risks. How can the legislature as a whole control its own agents—the committees—who are more active and knowledgeable than their principals, the entire legislature? This is the principal-agent problem discussed in chapter 1. And if the committees dominate legislative outcomes, does not this subvert the legislature's ability to represent the absent others? The integrity and cohesion of the political parties are also threatened by the committees; once assigned to a Storting committee, party members disappear into committee rooms to work long hours behind closed doors with members of the other parties in a setting that rewards compromise and consensus-seeking. Seventy-nine percent of all nonbudget committee recommendations between 1945 and 1989 were unanimous (Rommetvedt; 1992, 88–89), so there is a genuine risk of members being co-opted into a committee perspective that may diverge from their party's program or the preferences of the chambers as a whole.

Several features of the Storting seem to mitigate these dangers. Careful attention to committee personnel by the legislative and party leaders may substantially reduce the risk of agents controlling principals, rather than vice versa. The first stage in this process is the determination of the number of seats on each committee to be assigned to each party. This is worked out through negotiations between the party leaders after each election. They also decide which party is to supply the committee chair and other committee officers. Proportionality is the rule: the percentage of all seats parties control in the Storting is followed closely in allocating committee seats. The committee chairmanships are also allocated proportionally.[3] There is no rule or tradition of over-representing government parties in chairmanships or on important committees as there is in some other legislatures, such as the U.S. Congress. The major complicat-

Table 9.8

Members' Preferences and Committee Assignments

Committee	% of Membership Preferring Current Assignment	% of Those Preferring Committee but Not Serving on Committee in 1985–89
Foreign Affairs	100	83
Industry	100	81
Finance	93	80
Local Government	89	86
Fisheries	87.5	42
Social Affairs	77	71
Communications	71	89
Education	70	76
Agriculture	63.5	29
Judiciary	50	70
Defense	37.5	83
Administration	25	60

Note: Preferred committee assignments are those listed as among the members' top three preferences.

ing factor in pursuing the strategy of strict proportionality is the parties—the Socialist Left and Progress parties in 1985—that are too small to be represented on all ten committees.

Officially members are assigned to committees for four-year terms by an Elections Committee. In reality, each party group decides how to allocate its committee positions. This process, despite its obvious importance and potentially conflictual nature, has yet to be studied carefully. We can, however, make some tentative inferences about the criteria of choice that seem to be utilized.

The members' preferences are clearly taken into account in making committee assignments. In table 9.8 we present the percentage of committee members in 1985 who preferred the committee upon which they served. The committees are mostly made up of people who want to be there. Most committees include a few members who would prefer to serve elsewhere, and a few committees—Judiciary, Defense, and Administration—consist mostly of draftees.

This presumably leads to more eager, hard-working, and informed committees than would be the case if members' preferences were not considered. But this practice may also result in unrepresentative committees; members who want to serve on a committee are probably more interested in and knowledgeable about that committee's policy area than their colleagues who are not. Their constituents are likely to be more interested as well. Thus the Agriculture Committee attracts farmers from rural districts, Fisheries attracts members from areas in which fishing is a central concern, and so on. This is a major pattern in the committees in the United States Congress, resulting in sometimes significant tensions between the committees and their parent bodies, the House and the Senate.

Seniority is also a factor in committee assignments, although less so in the Storting than in many other legislatures. Reappointments to the same committee are common but far from automatic. In fact, committee personnel is far less stable than is the membership of the Storting as a whole. In the early 1980s more than 60 percent of Storting members were re-elected but fewer than 30 percent of committee members served two consecutive terms on the same committee. The 1989 elections shook up the people in the Storting—the re-election rate fell to 57 percent— but impacted the committees even more: carryovers from the previous term dropped to only 13 percent. Again there are interesting differences among the committees on this. The high-prestige committees—especially Foreign Affairs and Finance—have relatively slow turnover, as do Fisheries, Agriculture, and Local Government. The committees seen by members as undesirable—Administration, Defense, Judiciary—are staffed by members who rarely if ever return to them. Committees that turn over rapidly are not likely to develop expertise; those with stable memberships may be expert but can prove unresponsive and unrepresentative. Most Storting committees combine frequent membership turnover with a few longer-serving members. This is different than the American pattern where committee members serve indefinitely on the same committee.

While committees populated by members who want to serve on that committee tend to have atypical memberships, posing greater risks of shirking (the agent not doing what the principal wants), the personnel in the committees near the bottom of the pecking order is more representative of the entire chamber. Another consequence of the difference in committee popularity may have contrary effects. Eighty-three percent of those who would like to serve on Foreign Affairs are *not* members of the committee (table 9.8). This means that the work of the committee and others like it probably receives more interested and informed scrutiny from outside the committee than Agriculture or Fisheries or Administration where most of the members interested in the subject serve on the committee. The desirable and "important" committees are likely to have more active and informed critics within the legislature.

A second feature of the Storting that seems to mitigate against committee shirking is the regular monitoring of the committees and their work by the legislative parties. The parties assign members to committees as their representatives. Members of the committees report back to the parliamentary group, and there are debates in the party group over what policy stance these representatives should take in committee and how they should act. Committee members play a major role in these debates—they are better informed and more interested than most of their fellow partisans. But given the great power the political parties have over the careers of parliamentarians in Norway, the parties retain much control over their members' committee behavior.

Do the committee assignment processes, the practice of considerable rotation of members on committees, and the monitoring of the committees by the parties keep the committees from becoming laws unto themselves? How representative of the whole Parliament are the committees?

First, we shall compare the social composition of the committees with the composition of the Storting by dichotomizing the committee members and all other members of the Storting on the basis of their gender, occupational class, education, age, father's occupational class, place of residence, and place of birth. In table 9.9 we present the percentage point divergence between the committee membership and the entire Storting on all seven of these dimensions. There are some intriguing differences. Foreign Affairs, Local Government, Agriculture, Defense, Communications, and Industry are all more male than they would be if selected randomly. Education, Social Affairs, Fisheries, and Administration are more female. There still seems to be some tendency to gender-stereotype policy areas—education and social welfare policy are "female" topics, while economic issues and foreign/military policy are "male." But none of these differences is large enough to be statistically significant, even when the level of significance is set high (at $p \leq .10$) because of the small numbers involved. Basically, the committees are representative in their distribution of men and women members.

There is some tendency for the two most prestigious committees—Finance and Foreign Affairs—to have members of higher socioeconomic status, and for these two committees plus Industry to have more urban backgrounds than the rest of the chamber. This is consistent with Ottar

Table 9.9

Committee Members' Characteristics Compared to Those of Other Members, 1985–1989
(in Percentage Point Differences)

Committee	Male	Higher Occupation	University Education	40+	Father's High Occupation	Residence Urban	Birth Urban
Finance	+1.0	+6.5	+11.9	-9.0	-4.8	+12.5	+3.2
Foreign Affairs	+10.4	+16.3	+15.2	+4.7	+18.1	+44.2*	+23.9
Judiciary	+1.6	-23.8	+6.2	-15.2	+2.0	+4.3	+10.5
Administration	-2.9	+11.2	-11.4	+6.7	+9.0	-5.7	-0.8
Education	-27.2	-6.5	+31.6*	-1.3	+9.3	-28.0	+10.8
Local Government	+13.5	-12.5	+18.3	-6.6	+4.7	-22.3	-16.7
Agriculture	+13.5	+35.5*	-41.3*	+8.3	+21.3	-35.5*	-29.2
Defense	+10.4	+6.9	+1.9	-20.0	-1.0	+17.6	+10.6
Communications	+10.4	+1.2	+1.9	-20.0	-8.6	-22.2	-15.9
Fisheries	-2.9	+32.6*	-38.0*	-6.6	+4.7	-22.2	-15.9
Industry	+10.8	-6.6	+6.5	+2.3	-8.9	+22.8	+11.0
Social Affairs	-4.1	-10.9	-7.7	-38.8*	-19.6	+17.2	+6.9

*$p \leq .10$ using chi-square test with Yeates correction for small numbers.

Hellevik's findings some years ago (1969). But it should be noted that only one of the differences—the greater urbanity of Foreign Affairs members—is statistically significant. Overall, as might be expected, the Agriculture and Fisheries committees diverge the most from the chamber in their member characteristics. The Education Committee has far more university-educated members than its proportionate share, and the Social Affairs Committee is much younger than it would be if randomly selected. But the main conclusion that jumps out from table 9.9 is that the committees tend to reflect the social composition of the Storting quite well.

Second, do the committees represent the Storting in public policy terms? We compared the average (mean) issue position scores of members of the committees with all other Storting members on the same eighteen issues we utilized in earlier chapters. This resulted in 216 comparisons of mean scores. In only eighteen cases were the differences statistically significant (at $p \leq .10$).

But the performance is actually better than this. We compared the policy views of all committees with the Storting on all eighteen issues. But we are primarily interested in how representative committee views are in the area of their jurisdiction, since this is where the committees have power. In table 9.10, we list the eighteen cases in which a committee diverged from the remainder of the Storting at statistically significant leads. Only seven of these occurred within the committees' general area of jurisdiction. In 1985–89, the Finance Committee was more opposed to cutting the public sector, while the Industry Committee was more favorable to reducing public expenditures than the Storting. As a whole, the Local Government Committee (concerned with housing and environmental issues) was in favor of more and easier home loans and more environmental protection than its colleagues. The Agriculture Committee wanted more financial aid to the rural periphery than the others. The Defense Committee was predictably more in favor of stronger national defense and more opposed to forbidding atomic weapons than the rest of the legislature. All the other differences in policy positions between committees and the Storting were either unimportant, because they were outside the committees' areas of concern, or not statistically significant. With these few exceptions, the committees were representative of the entire Storting in policy terms. The principal-agent problems created by the committee system seems under control.

Table 9.10

Issue Positions of Committees and Other Members, 1985

Committee	Issue	Mean Issue Scores		2-tailed p
		Committee	Other Members	
Finance	**Cut public sector**	3.79	3.22	.01
Foreign Affairs	Strengthen urban economies	2.62	3.34	.03
Administration	Forbid private hospitals	3.87	2.63	.09
Education	Reduce state regulation	4.00	3.69	.09
	Reduce immigration	4.00	3.48	.01
Local Government	Forbid atomic weapons	2.00	2.49	.08
	More home loans	1.44	1.83	.06
	Environmental protection	1.33	1.68	.08
Agriculture	More sexual equality	1.25	1.70	.03
	Aid to periphery	1.62	2.25	.10
Defense	**Strengthen national defense**	1.25	3.57	.01
	Forbid atomic weapons	3.57	2.41	.02
	Environmental protection	2.12	1.63	.07
Communications	Reduce state regulation	4.12	3.68	.10
Fisheries	Aid to developing countries	2.14	2.50	.09
Industry	Aid to developing countries	3.08	2.43	.05
	Reduce public expenditures	2.42	2.97	.04
	Reduce immigration	2.67	3.60	.01

Notes: Scores range from 1.0 (favorable to stated position) to 5.0 (unfavorable). Boldface indicates that the issue falls within the committee's jurisdiction.

Group Communications and Policy-Making

Norway is one of the most thoroughly organized societies in the world. Groups and associations of every conceivable sort are packed into this small and seemingly homogeneous land. The relationships between these groups and the state are usually described as neo-corporatist; that is, private groups tend to be formally and officially incorporated into the governmental process. Most of the attention of scholars has been directed at these corporatist connections during the pre- or post-legislative stages of policy-making. In seeking to extend this perspective to the Storting, we have so far discussed the group bases of the political parties and their nominations to the Storting. Many groups are represented in the Storting indirectly through the various parties and directly by group members elected to the chamber. But do groups and associations play any additional part in the Storting's representation of the Norwegian people? The answer is an emphatic "yes."

In our 1985 Storting study, we asked the members to report the frequency of their written or oral contacts with twenty-four different categories of organizations (coincidental meetings and news stories were not counted). The results are presented in table 9.11. The quantity and range of communications between Storting members and the nation's groups and associations is astonishing. Twenty-eight percent of the members reported daily or weekly contacts with the Norwegian Federation of Trade Unions (LO) and its affiliated organizations; more than 60 percent reported LO contacts at least monthly. No other group or category was quite so well connected, but groups of teachers, students, and researchers; young people; industry associations; social and humanitarian associations; and organizations dedicated to environmental protection and the interests of women were in contact with 40 percent or more of the Storting at least once a month. Even small and arcane organizations communicate with some members of the national legislature on a moderately frequent basis.

Our questionnaire results do not tell us who initiated the contacts, although their great volume strongly suggests that the busy members do not initiate most of them. Nor do we know the content of the messages, although it seems safe to assume that not many of them are casual conversations about the weather or other matters unrelated to the Storting members' official duties. Those duties, of course, involve more than legislating, narrowly defined, and include the provision of services to constituents. So it would be a mistake to conclude that all the contacts

Table 9.11

Members' Frequency of Contact with Types of Organizations (%)

| | Frequency of Contact | | | | |
Types of Group	Daily/ Weekly	Monthly	Seldom/ Never	Total	N
LO and affiliates	28	35	37	100	145
Teachers, students, researchers	21	37	43	100	145
Youth	12	45	43	100	143
Industry	12	43	45	100	145
Social and humanitarian	16	36	48	100	146
Environmental	13	36	51	100	144
Women	16	24	60	100	144
Banking and insurance	12	28	60	100	146
Transportation and communications	16	24	60	100	142
Employees (outside LO)	6	32	62	100	146
Foreign policy and defense	12	25	63	100	144
Employers	6	29	65	100	144
Sports and recreation	6	29	65	100	143
Agriculture and forestry	8	27	65	100	141
Language, arts, and culture	14	19	67	100	143
Fishing	9	23	68	100	141
Business	5	26	69	100	144
Retired persons	5	25	70	100	146
Tourism, travel, hotels	8	22	70	100	145
Consumers	4	25	71	100	143
Housing, property owners	5	20	75	100	144
Temperance	5	17	78	100	143
Religions	9	10	81	100	144
Shipping	4	11	85	100	145

concern policy issues. Despite these important caveats, table 9.11 shows who the Storting communicates with and how often. This tells us much about who has the most, and least, access to the national legislature through organizational channels. Access is not necessarily power, but it is both a necessary condition for, and usually a consequence of, power.

The Storting's communications with organizations are shaped both by the political parties and the Storting's committee system. Let us look at each of these influences in turn.

Members of different parties tend to communicate with different

Table 9.12
% in Contact with Organizations At Least Once per Month, by Party

Type of Group	Parties				All Members
	DNA	SP	KrF	H	
LO and affiliates	93	27	38	31	63
Teachers, students, researchers	53	73	50	62	57
Youth	60	64	54	56	57
Industry	48	55	62	67	55
Social and humanitarian	52	55	69	51	52
Environmental	56	45	46	38	49
Women	54	27	38	24	40
Banking and insurance	31	55	40	44	40
Transportation and communications	44	45	46	29	40
Employees (outside LO)	34	45	29	43	38
Foreign policy and defense	29	36	36	56	37
Employers	30	45	36	44	35
Sports and recreation	37	54	46	24	35
Agriculture and forestry	32	82	23	32	35
Language, arts, and culture	26	27	46	43	33
Fishing	32	18	46	19	32
Business	23	54	38	35	31
Retired persons	37	18	36	21	30
Tourism, travel, hotels	27	45	15	40	30
Consumers	38	27	31	15	29
Housing, property owners	30	27	23	19	25
Temperance	19	36	57	12	23
Religions	7	18	70	22	19
Shipping	14	27	21	12	15

Note: Socialist Left and Progress Parties omitted due to small numbers.

groups at different rates (see table 9.12). Ninety-three percent of the Labor Party members are in frequent contact (at least once a month) with
LO; 70 percent of the members of the Christian People's Party are in frequent contact with religious groups; 82 percent of the Center Party with
agricultural groups, and so on. These groups not only vote for these
parties, but are in close communications with these Storting members
between elections. To some extent, then, the structure of group communications with the Storting mirrors the group basis of the political parties.

But group communications with the Storting contains far more than that. Most of the groups in tables 9.11 and 12 have no ties with the political parties. These groups communicate with members without much regard for their party affiliations—teachers and students, young people, social and humanitarian groups are a few examples. Moreover, organizations closely allied with one party communicate with members of other parties to a surprising degree. Thus, 31 percent of Høyre members report they are in close touch with LO, and 30 percent of the Labor members report close contacts with employers associations, 31 percent report close contacts with banking and insurance organizations, 23 percent with business groups, and so on.

Communications between organizations and the legislature provide a more detailed, complex, and nuanced set of messages than political parties (even six of them) can.

The Committee system affects the flow of communications to the Storting more than the parties do. In table 9.13, the organizations most often in contact with the members of the various committees are listed. The dominant pattern is that organizations tend to focus their communications on the members of committees dealing with matters of special concern to them. While this is an understandable and probably unavoidable practice, it means that the Storting committees hear more from those with immediate interest in their deliberations and less from those with more diffuse, indirect, or distant concerns. The potential for committee decisions biased in favor of the immediate parties at interest rather than the general interest is obvious.

There are, however, a number of organizations that communicate with the Storting on a wide range of issue areas. LO, for example, is one of the top five organizations in communications with all but one of the committees. Youth groups are also highly vocal; they are among the top five sources of communications in eight different committees. Women's groups and environmental organizations also communicate at high rates with many committees.

Groups and associations tend to contact members of the Storting with whom they agree. For example, in table 9.14 we compare the issue scores of members who are frequently (at least monthly) in contact with LO and those members who are not on eighteen different policy issues. The mean scores of these two groups are different in seventeen of these eighteen issues. And those members in frequent contact with LO tend to agree with LO positions. Does this mean that this communication between LO and the members caused this agreement? Maybe sometimes, but mostly

Table 9.13

Top Five Organizations Contacting Storting Committees (in % of Committee Members in Contact Monthly or More Often)

Finance	Foreign Affairs	Industry
Banking and insurance (79)	Foreign affairs/military (75)	Trade and industry (83)
Trade and industry (71)	Youth (75)	LO (75)
Youth (61.5)	Humanitarian/social (62.5)	Youth (58)
LO (57)	Teachers, students, researchers (62.5)	Employers (outside LO) (50)
Employers, consumers, humanitarian/social (43)	LO (50)	Environmental, overseas and military, humanitarian/social (42)

Defense	Education	Agriculture
Foreign affairs/military (100)	Arts and culture (100)	Transportation and communications (100)
Youth (75)	Environmental (60)	Youth (100)
Sports (57)	Humanitarian/social (60)	Agriculture and forestry (87.5)
Humanitarian/social (62.5)	Women (60)	Trade and industry (87.5)
LO (50)	Youth (60)	LO (75)

continued

Table 9.13
continued

Administration	Judiciary	Fisheries
Banking and insurance (71)	Youth (67)	Fishing (87.5)
Teachers, students, researchers (62.5)	Retirees (67)	Shipping (75)
LO (62.5)	Teachers, students, researchers (67)	LO (57)
Consumers (43)	LO (50)	Transportation and communications (43)
Business, environmental, arts and culture (43)	Trade and industry, consumers, environmental, humanitarian/social, women (50)	Women (43)

Local Government	Communications	Social Affairs
Environmental (89)	Transportation and communications (87.5)	Humanitarian/social (100)
LO (78)	Youth (71)	LO (77)
Youth (78)	Trade and industry (67.5)	Employers (outside LO) (61.5)
Fishing (67)	Tourism (62.5)	Environmental (54)
Employers, humanitarian/social (67)	LO (58)	Temperance; retirees; teachers, students, researchers (54)

not. A more plausible explanation for this pattern is that both LO and the members tend to communicate with their political friends. Since LO is formally associated with the largest party in the Storting, it has many friends. Groups frequently remind their friends in the Storting of their interests and seek to help them become effective advocates of positions they both support. Members who have little staff support call upon interested and friendly organizations for information and advice on policy matters.

LO, of course, is not the only organization that has this pattern of communication. Women, industrial groups, and consumers groups also seem to communicate predominantly with supporters—members they frequently contact differ sharply from those they rarely contact (see table 9.15). To a somewhat lesser degree, so do foreign affairs, environmental, employers, travel, religious, and retail business organizations.

While this may be the predominate pattern of contacts between private associations and members of the Storting, there are many others. Groups with small memberships or narrow interests or unpopular opinions have too few friends in the Storting to rely upon them alone. Teachers, students, and youth groups are among the most active groups, but there are few policy differences between Storting members they contact and those they do not. Banking associations, employee groups (not in LO), fishing, temperance, and shipping groups are much less active but also lack distinct followings in the Storting. This is not convincing evidence of political ineffectiveness, but it does suggest that possibility.

Conclusions

In this chapter we have sought to examine some ways in which the organization, rules, and procedures of the Storting affect how it represents the absent others. While we have scarcely exhausted the subject, we have identified several significant findings.

1. What being a representative means is partially defined by the members. Members have some choice over what to represent—the party, the district, different groups and interests within party and district. They also decide how to allocate their time between committee work, party work, servicing the district, and other responsibilities. Those choices are shaped by each member's personal background, the circumstances of his or her nomination, committee assignments, and other offices held within

Table 9.14

Contacts with LO and Issue Positions of Storting Members (Mean Issue Scores)

Issue	At Least Monthly	Seldom or Never	Statistical Significance of Difference in Mean Position
Strengthen defense	2.09	1.42	.000
Equality between sexes	1.53	1.89	.016
Abolish grading in secondary schools	3.14	4.38	.000
Strengthen Christian morals	3.05	2.14	.000
Equalization between social groups	1.48	2.21	.000
Prohibit atomic weapons	1.58	3.26	.000
Lower taxes	1.22	1.19	.000
Lower interest on housing loans	1.60	2.15	.000
More economic support to periphery	1.04	2.49	.013
End state regulation of business	4.00	3.23	.000
Environmental protection	1.63	1.72	.465
Aid to developing countries	2.23	2.96	.000
Stop growth of public sector	3.37	2.19	.000
Prohibit private hospitals	2.18	3.53	.000
Expand public sector to secure full employment	2.91	3.85	.000
Strengthen economies of big cities	3.09	3.62	.000
More nursery schools	1.91	2.78	.000
Restrict admission of refugees	3.64	3.30	.049

Note: Issue scores range from 1.0 (entirely in favor of position) to 5.0 (entirely opposed).

the Storting. Service in the Storting is an educational experience—members develop new skills and orientations. Most members become more interested in and sophisticated about national and international issues and gravitate toward the committees that deal with those subjects as their years of service continue. A minority of the members, however, remain local politicians at heart and spend their time dealing with relatively parochial matters. The leadership of the Storting (and ultimately the country) comes from the first group.[4]

2. The standing committees in the Storting are unusually strong for a parliamentary system. Much of most members' time and energy is devoted to committee work. The committees make it possible for the Stor-

Table 9.15

Difference between Policy Views of Storting Members with Frequent
Contact with Associations and Those With Little Contact

Type of Association	% of Time Differences Are Statistically Significant ($p \leq .05$)
LO	94
Women's organizations	83
Industry	67
Consumers	61
Foreign affairs/military affairs	44
Environmental groups	39
Employers associations	39
Tourism, travel, hotels	39
Religious/Christian associations	33
Retirees	28
Housing and property owners	17
Agriculture and forestry	11
Sports	11
Language, arts, and culture	11
Business	11
Humanitarian and social	6
Transportation and communications	6
Teachers, students, researchers; youth; banking and insurance; employees (not LO); fishing; temperance; shipping	0

Note: Differences are on eighteen policy issues. Frequent contacts = monthly or
more often.

ting to do more than debate and then merely ratify government
proposals. But they also pose problems for a representative legislature.
Committees can develop their own policy perspectives. How can a legislature control its own agents—the committees—who are more active and
knowledgeable than their principals, the entire legislature?

The committee assignment process, which is essentially controlled by
the party groups, seems to be one key to this puzzle. So are the fairly
frequent rotation of members among the committees and the close monitoring of the committees by the legislative parties. Members understand-
ably want to serve on committees that contribute to their goals. But a few
committees are very popular while others are not, and everyone cannot

get his or her preference. Moreover, those who want to serve on a committee are frequently a skewed sample of the legislature. Somehow, the parties manage to resolve these problems so that the committees tend to be representative of the entire Storting in terms of both the social characteristics of committee members and their policy views. There are some interesting differences in the backgrounds and perspectives of committees and the parent chamber but they are surprisingly few.

3. The quantity and range of communications between the Storting and the nation's myriad groups and organization are impressive. Clearly, these groups play a part in the legislative process as well as in policy initiative and implementation and party politics. Communications between organizations and the Storting provide a more detailed, complex, and nuanced set of messages than the political parties do. We suggest that the frequency with which the Storting hears from different organizations and associations provides a picture of who has access to the Storting.

But access does not equal power—some groups communicate with the Storting frequently without much apparent effect. The design of our research does not allow us to study the effects of group communications directly. We do examine whether or not those members of the Storting in close communication with a group differ in their policy views from those members of the Storting not in communication with the same group. Some groups—the Norwegian Federation of Trade Unions, women's organizations, and industrial groups, for example—tend to communicate with those members they agree with. Other groups—teachers and students, young people, temperance groups—lack distinct followings in the Storting and end up communicating with everyone. The first type of group emphasizes mobilizing friends, the second type is still looking for them.

10

Conclusions

T his book began with a question: How and how well does the Norwegian Storting represent the Norwegian people? The time has come to sum up what we have found. We shall look at policy, symbolic, and service representation separately.

Policy Representation

Storting majorities usually, but not always, agree with a majority of the voters on public policy issues. This is the bottom line of policy representation. How this agreement between the Storting and the absent others occurs has been the major concern of this book. But we must not forget that achieving such agreement is a major accomplishment.

About 85 percent of the Norwegian electorate are inactive, uninvolved, and poorly informed about politics. This is a regrettable departure from conventional assumptions about political democracy. But Norway is not alone in possessing disinterested and inactive citizens. This pattern is the norm among democratic countries, not the exception.

There are two schools of thought about the inactivity and lack of political involvement of ordinary democratic citizens. One approach argues that the people shun politics because they are alienated, cynical, and powerless. The alternative approach argues that the inactive citizens do not engage in politics because they are satisfied with how they are being governed. In Norway, the second explanation is the more persuasive for most people. Certainly, alienation and cynicism exist in Norway to some degree. But politically inactive Norwegians possess the same high level of trust in government as do the politically active. And the most disinterested Norwegians vote at very high levels! Passive acquiescence seems to characterize the inactive 85 percent.

The 15 percent (more or less) of the Norwegian electorate who are active, involved and informed about Norwegian politics become a surrogate for the entire electorate by default—subject only to continued mass acquiescence and periodic elections. This group is open to all, a self-selected elite. Men more often than women become activists, as do older people. The educational and occupational levels of the activists, however, do not diverge significantly from those of the inactive citizens. As a group their policy views tend to be a little closer to those of Storting members than the rank and file.

Much of Norwegian politics consists of the active minority, including members of the Storting, trying to anticipate what the interests and preferences of the quiescent are, or might become in the future. This, of course, provides many opportunities for leadership—members of the active minority attempting to persuade the inactive majority to adopt their views. It also provides opportunities for the failure of representation.

Of course the active minority are of several minds about many things, so there is competition among the activists for mass approval and support. Political parties simplify and structure this competition. They define the options that the inactive and disinterested voters choose between. The proportional representation electoral system, with a low threshold of votes needed to win a seat in the Storting, combined with state subsidies, ensures that there are a number of parties. If a significant set of people, interests, or ideas is ignored by the established parties, new parties emerge, as did the Labor Party in 1887, the Farmers' Party/ Center Party in 1920, the Christian People's Party in 1933, the Socialist People's Party in 1961 (which became the Socialist Left in 1975), and the Progress Party in 1973. Of course, the dissatisfied may choose to express themselves through nonparty groups or political movements, protests, and other less conventional behavior.

Despite the central importance of political parties in Norway the party mandate model of representation is a distortion of their role. The voters' feelings about the parties, based upon their past performance, is more important in shaping their votes than contemporary issues. On contemporary issues there is not much agreement within the parties beyond a few core issues about which they strongly agree. The Storting's consensual style of decision-making further erodes the significance of party mandates. Thus policy mandates about future issues are seldom clear, although winners routinely claim mandates to do what they want.

How elections are organized has significant effects on the process of representation. Since the adoption of PR in 1919, the political parties have received approximately their proportionate share of the seats in the Storting, but the larger parties still receive a few more seats than their arithmetic due. Much larger distortions, however, are introduced by the use of the province (fylke) as the electoral unit and the apportionment of seats to the fylker so as to over-represent the peripheral far North and Southwest and to under-represent Oslo and surrounding areas. We estimate, for example, that the net result of electoral system distortions in the 1985 election was to increase the Labor Party's ranks in the Storting from sixty-four to seventy-one seats. The Conservatives gained two extra seats, the Christians three, and the Center Party two. All the other parties received fewer seats than their voters would justify.

A party-based explanation of the agreement between the Storting and the voters overlooks the linkages provided by nonparty groups in Norwegian politics. Norway is one of the most highly organized societies in the world. Some of the larger groups are affiliated with the political parties, but most are not. They send strong, continuous, and highly nuanced messages to the members of the Storting about policy matters.

Democratic government can be thought of as a giant principal-agent problem. Most of the time the agents (the members of the Storting) do what the voters (the principals) want without the voters paying much attention. But the Storting and the voters do not always and invariably agree. There are some issues and circumstances where the Storting systematically diverges from the preponderate views of the absent others.

1. *Foreign and military policies.* The Storting in recent decades has been more internationalist, more favorably inclined toward NATO and the European Union, than the Norwegian electorate. Twice during this period, the Storting has favored entering the EU, and twice these initiatives have been defeated by popular votes in national referenda. Storting majorities have not yet succeeded in leading the country in a more internationalist direction.

2. *New issues.* New problems and new issues pose both opportunities and risks to established political parties and the Storting. The Liberal Party was shattered by the EC issue and came back years later as the most vocal advocate of environmental protection. Most of the other parties followed Liberal's lead and Norway was spared a strong greens (anti)party as in Sweden and Germany (Aardal, 1990). The issue of gender equality took a long time to arrive on the nation's agenda. The Socialist Left and Labor parties took the lead and thereby strengthened their support among women voters even after all the other parties (except the Progress Party) joined them in support of equality for women. Thus parties

respond to new issues and problems in different ways that can have significant consequences for representation.

3. *Statism.* The Storting as a whole shows greater confidence in government as a problem solver than do the rank-and-file voters. This is not just the result of the over-representation of the Labor Party; the tendency exists within all the parties. Privatization, reduced government, and reliance on markets for the allocation of goods and services are more popular outside the Storting than within it.

4. *Extremism.* A number of studies have found that the party leaders are more ideologically extreme—be it of the left or right—than their followers (Rabinowitz, 1978; Dalton, 1985; Holmberg, 1989; Rabinowitz and Macdonald, 1989; Rabinowitz, Macdonald, and Listhaug, 1991; Iversen, 1994). Our data show that this is true for Storting members. However, when we compare the policy views of all voters with the policy views of all members of the Storting, we do not find over-representation of the ideological extremes. In 1985 at least, the errors in representation within the parties cancel out when they are combined in the legislative body.

Symbolic Representation

The members of the Norwegian Parliament are unusually similar, in personal terms, to the people they represent. Even so, the Storting is scarcely a mirror image of Norwegian society; its members tend more often to be male, wealthier, and better educated and have more prestigious jobs than the average Norwegian. These biases in the recruitment of legislators seem to exist in all modern, representative systems. The Storting, however, is one of the most egalitarian and hence representative of all national legislatures. Probably the biggest difference between the members of the Storting and the absent others is that the members are mostly experienced, elective officeholders before their election.

The social and economic inclusiveness of the Storting did not come quickly or easily. It took a century and a half for the Storting to evolve from a legislature dominated by civil servants, businessmen, and professional men to today's mix of people. The rate and extent of these changes in the social profile of the Storting cannot be explained by the spread of democratic ideals and the expansion of the suffrage alone. The United States, for example, embraced democratic ideals and a mass electorate at about the same time as Norway without opening the doors to the Congress very significantly.

Our explanation of the Storting's inclusiveness is primarily institutional. The combination of PR elections, electoral districts with large magnitudes, and party nomination made by local party leadership groups chosen at open conventions tends to provide easier access to Storting seats for previously unrepresented groups than do other kinds of electoral arrangements. A politician in Norway does not run for the Storting as an individual but as part of a party list. The local party activists who put the lists together tend to develop balanced lists that they see as increasing the chance of victory while reducing internal conflict within the party. Local nominating meetings are poorly attended and are susceptible to capture by people who feel left out. Including newcomers on electoral lists often seems more sensible than risking a bruising fight.

The social and economic characteristics of members of the Storting is one form of symbolic representation. There are many others—most activities of the Storting and its members have a symbolic aspect. Symbolic representation aims to engender respect for the institution and acquiescence to its decisions. While the Storting, along with other national legislatures, has come under criticism in recent decades, the Storting tends to be seen as at least as praiseworthy and deserving of trust as other political institutions in Norway and is far more favorably evaluated than most other national legislatures.

Service Representation

Virtually all members of the Storting report that they try to promote the interests of their district within the Storting and in the executive departments. Most members return to the districts frequently; more than half spend ten days or more per month in their districts. They are in regular and frequent contact with local party leaders (crucial in slate-making) and officials at the municipal and provincial levels. The second most popular reason among Storting members for desiring a specific committee assignment is that the assignment would do the most for the member's district. (The most popular reason for desiring a specific committee assignment is that it would lead to more influence in the Storting.) A sizable minority of the Storting—especially those from the far North and Southwest—are district-oriented.

These behaviors are often ignored in studies of representation, since they do not seem to have much to do with public policy. Much of this takes place far from Oslo and is seldom covered by the media. But members of the Storting are prominent and influential members of local political and social systems. They are expected to champion local interests, big and small, within their parties, in the halls of the Storting, in committee rooms, at the departments. This aspect of legislative representation needs more attention than we have been able to give it.

Beyond the Storting

Does this study of the Norwegian national legislature lead to a better understanding of political representation in general? Readers will have to decide this question for themselves. But we cannot resist summarizing what we hope this case study may have contributed to the understanding of representation in other settings.

1. We believe that students of representation need to adopt a broader view of the subject and to develop more complex and realistic models than those which have guided much of our thinking to date.

2. In this book we have tried to focus on the process of representation, isolating institutions and practices that tend to encourage or discourage agreement between the representatives and the represented. The responses of the two sides of this relationship to each other are not immediate but usually take some time—sometimes years—to work themselves out. A single sample survey provides a snapshot; what we need is a moving picture, both of mass preferences and the behavior of representatives.

3. Our approach has led us to stress the importance of the electoral system and the nomination of candidates to subsequent legislative representation. The electoral system impacts the representation of parties and geographical areas in the legislature in predictable ways; there is a growing body of sophisticated analyses of this phenomenon (Grofman and Lijphart, 1986). But the electoral system also affects the type of persons elected and their behavior once in office. We have hazarded a few ideas on both these things. We also suggest that electoral systems are constantly revised so their effects are not constant. And finally we point out that nominations may be more important than general elections in conditioning how representation works, perhaps especially in PR-list systems when the voting strength of the parties is relatively stable.

4. Finally, we stress the importance of the active minority in Norwegian democracy, and we believe this is also true in other systems. We do not advocate an elitist theory of democracy, but merely argue that such an active minority seems critically important in the absence of active

and well-informed citizenry. The puzzle of representative democracy remains. How can a political system be devised in which the inactive, disinterested, and modestly informed citizens control the broad outlines of government policy? In these pages we have tried to describe the Norwegian solution.

Developments since 1985

The analysis presented in this book is based primarily upon data from 1985. One may wonder: Are the results still valid? To what extent has the process of representation changed during the subsequent years? Norwegian politics has become more turbulent and volatile, a tendency that has affected executive-legislative relations.

The 1985 election resulted in a deadlock. The three bourgeois coalition parties lost their majority and returned with jointly seventy-eight seats; the opposition parties of the left obtained seventy-seven seats; and the right-wing Progress Party with its two seats arrived in a pivotal position. Since then, the Progress Party has increased its size and maintained a balancing position between the bourgeois parties and the two parties of the left. Moreover, the former coalition parties have been severely split due to the issue of EU membership, which has dominated Norwegian politics in the 1990s. As a consequence, the two-bloc system has broken down. Since 1985 the country has been run by minority governments, most of the time by Labor. Although there is a long tradition for minority parliamentarism in Norway, in recent years it has become more difficult to maintain viable governments.

Unable to form a new government alternative, the competing opposition parties are inclined to promote their own separate policy solutions. At recent elections the governing Labor Party has lost in strength. Aware of the critical parliamentary situation, the government has had to pay a high price for establishing temporary Storting majorities. In fact, the government has been forced to accept a number of defeats in the Storting. As a consequence the power of the Storting has increased at the cost of the executive branch.

This development has possibly increased the ability of political parties to maneuver in the parliamentary arena, but roll call analysis indicates that the role of the individual Storting member in relation to his or her party is basically unaffected.

With relevance to political accountability, however, the result may be different. According to the principal-agent model, accountability may be defined in terms of the ability of the principal to induce the agent to act in the principal's interests. In order to do so, and in order to distinguish beneficial from detrimental actions, the principal needs information about the agent's actions. In a situation of clear-cut government alternatives, which was the case two decades ago, and in situations with shifting majority solutions, the electorate (i.e., the ultimate principal) is likely to be relatively well-informed about policies and political actions of different parties (the agents). Moreover, the high level of turnout as well as the expressed trust in government in the 1985 study indicates that at this time the principal was confident in leaving the decision-making to the agents.

In the current minority situation, on the other hand, where parliamentary horse-trading is the norm, the voters' level of information is likely to be lower and political responsibility will be correspondingly blurred. Politics in recent years has been characterized by declining turnout and declining trust in government. Nobody can predict how long this situation is going to last, but the possibility of long-term effects on the process of representation calls for repeated studies of mass-elite linkages.

Our analysis has indicated that political activists constitute a relatively small proportion of the electorate. Recent research suggests that this proportion may have reached an even lower level since 1985, at least as far as the number of dues-paying party members is concerned. This tendency may have been provoked by current events. Thus, the divisive EU controversy caused frustrations among a great number of voters and made them break with their traditional party loyalties (Narud and Valen, 1996). Another equally interesting possibility is that the decline in political activism is affected by new campaign technologies, above all television.

A further decline in political activism implies a smaller elite of attentive and active citizens. The consequences of this for political representation are unknown. But the assumption that political parties as institutions will disappear from the system is inconceivable. The parliamentary form of government requires parties, or equivalent organizations, for the formulation of alternative policies and the recruitment of political leaders.

The Future

Change is one of the few certainties in politics. What will the Norwegian political system be like in the twenty-first century? What will happen to the complex arrangements that make up representative government,

Norwegian style? No one knows, of course. But we can point out several things that may trigger significant changes in the future.

1. Electoral politics is being transformed everywhere by new technologies—television, polling, computerized mass mailings, focus groups, and so on—and the emergence of new professionals expert at applying these technologies to politics. In the United States, where the trend has gone farther than anywhere, new political technologies have become controversial. Critics, often relying upon anecdotal evidence, argue that the new political technology has contributed to the rise to power of a new breed of politician more adept at self-promotion and television campaigning than governing (Ehrenhalt, 1991; Bennett, 1992); the decline of political parties and the rise of candidate-oriented, every-man-for-himself politics (Wattenberg, 1986); an alarming loss of civility and comity (Uslaner, 1993); and a reduced ability to aggregate votes, interests, and people into policy-making majorities (Burnham, 1982). No one argues that these ills are solely the results of the new political technologies. Rather, the argument is that when these techniques were introduced in the United States with its weak political parties, elective president, and separation of powers, they seemed to have these consequences.

There are some signs of the Americanization of Norwegian politics today. National politics is mostly television politics, personalities are more important in campaigns, the political parties are weaker than they used to be, and so on. But the thoroughgoing Americanization of Norwegian politics is not likely—the same technologies in the Norwegian context will not have the same consequences as in the United States. But they will change electoral politics in the future, and small changes in election processes and outcomes can have larger consequences for representation.

2. According to Edward Carmines and James Stimson, some political issues are "capable of altering the political environment within which they originated and evolved" (1989: 11). Carmines and Stimson call them "issue evolutions." Most issues capture the public's attention for too short a time—if at all—to lead to fundamental and permanent change. But issue evolutions do. Carmine and Stimson's example is the issue of race in the United States.

In contemporary Norwegian politics one issue seems to qualify as an issue evolution. That issue is Norway's relationship with the European Union. This emotional issue has been around at least since the 1960s (Allen, 1979). Referenda were held on the issue in 1972 and again in 1994. Both times the anti-Europeans won after bitter and divisive campaigns. The leader of both large parties (Labor and Conservatives) and of the most powerful and prestigious interest groups were on the losing side both times. The short-run impact of these emotion-packed events was substantial. The "establishment" was chastened and the Liberal Party split so badly that, for a time, it lost all its seats in the Storting. The Center Party was so strengthened that it won more seats than the Conservatives at the next general election. The Labor Party was—and remains—deeply divided on the issue. The issue is not settled; it will need to be dealt with again and again in the future. In the process, it may have large and permanent effects on Norwegian politics.

3. Norway's oil-based affluence cannot last forever. Since the end of World War II, Norway has moved from one of the poorest nations in Europe to one of the richest in the world, and North Sea oil has contributed substantially to this development. Governing is always easier when the pie to be divided is large and constantly increasing in size. Most modern democracies have experienced little or no economic growth in recent decades. As their populations grow older, the costs of their health and welfare programs soar, and so do the problems of those entrusted to govern. Tension between the young and the old takes on a seriousness previously reserved for class conflicts. When oil-based affluence declines, Norwegian political institutions and arrangements will be severely tested, and consensus may not come easily.

It would be a mistake to end this book on such an ominous note. Norway's representative, consensus-seeking style of democracy has survived many serious challenges in the past, including five years of military occupation by Nazi Germany. Judged by almost any standard, representative democracy in Norway has been very successful. There are many more reasons to feel confident about its future than apprehensive about problems dimly visible on the horizon.

Notes

Chapter 1

1. In the Middle Ages the *ting* was an assembly consisting of all free men, which met regularly and functioned partly as a legislative body and partly as a court. There were three regional tings in the country. The word Storting means the ting of the whole nation. In the saga period tings existed in some form or another in all Nordic countries (Ross, 1946). In our days the term is also preserved in the names of the parliaments of Iceland (Allting) and Denmark (Folketing).

2. Jewell (1985), Thomassen (1994), and Christophersen (1969) are excellent reviews of the literature. Here we shall merely comment upon works that have most influenced our thinking about the Storting.

3. The study has been reported by Aardal and Valen (1989). For details about sampling design, see Central Bureau of Statistics of Oslo (1986).

Chapter 2

1. The most important source was Magnus Lagaboter's law collection of 1276.

2. This prolonged battle was called the veto struggle (*vetostriden*). According to the Constitution the king had a so-called delaying veto in legal matters; i.e., he could twice refuse to sanction decisions by the Storting, but if the decision was upheld a third time, it became law without the royal consent. The Constitution specified this procedure for legal matters but did not mention constitutional amendments. The divisive debate in the 1870s focused upon the interpretation of the Constitution. The government, the Supreme Court, and other legal authorities held the position that since the Constitution failed to mention a veto regarding constitutional matters, it meant that the king had absolute veto in such matters. The liberal opposition drew the opposite conclusion: the king had no veto at all in constitutional matters. The Storting took an in-between course, behaving as if the king's delaying veto also covered constitutional amendments. Three times the Storting decided that members of the government should appear in the Storting. The government was impeached for not having complied after the Storting made the decision for the third time.

3. The term *bourgeois* is used as a general characterization of nonsocialist parties in Norway.

4. Venstre regained a parliamentary seat in 1993.

5. The full name of the party was "Anders Langes Party for strong reduction of taxes and public expenditure."

6. Party dues in 1996 were less than $25 per year in all the parties.

7. The figure was later raised to 2.5.

Chapter 3

1. For an overall view of current research on electoral systems, see Taagepera and Shugart (1989).

2. V. O. Key, Jr. (1949) points out that giving the vote to people who are otherwise powerless may not help them at all. The case Key studied so brilliantly was that of the former black slaves in the American South. Even after being granted the right to vote by the federal government, they were effectively disenfranchised by white Southerners for the better part of a century. See Matthews and Prothro (1966) for an analysis of how this condition finally was changed.

3. Since several cities and towns (sometimes from more than one province) had to be lumped together in the urban constituencies, the residents of the smaller, urban places complained of no effective representation under this arrangement.

4. The Listeforbund permitted two or more parties to have their votes counted jointly in specific constituencies, if this benefited their representation. The arrangement implied that surplus votes could be transferred from one party to another. This was beneficial for minor parties that were below the threshold of representation as well as for larger parties that did not have enough votes for obtaining another seat. By applying Listeforbund in several constituencies, the cooperating parties might be able to increase their representation.

5. Bergen remained a single constituency until 1965, when it was merged with the surrounding province of Hordaland.

6. According to the d'Hondt method, the total number of votes for a given party is divided successively by 1, 2, 3, 4, etc., after each seat obtained. The modified Sainte Laguë method prescribes that the votes be divided by 1.4 and subsequent odd numbers—1, 3, 5, 7, etc.—for each seat obtained. We present the results of the two different systems in the province of Hedmark at the 1985 Storting election. See the appendix to this chapter.

7. Observe that parties below this threshold may obtain representation in individual constituencies.

8. Very small political parties have been omitted in figuring this average. If they had been included the average deviation from the ideal figure would have been much larger.

Chapter 4

1. Arguably, architectural arrangements affect (and reflect) the style and substance of what happens within them. It is difficult to imagine the Norwegian Parliament at work within the Palace of Westminster or the U.S. Capitol, or to conceive of the British Parliament or American Congress conducting business in the (suitably enlarged) Storting building.

2. Since 1884 impeachment has been applied only once, in 1926.

3. Any bill is first presented in the Odelsting, which decides by a majority vote to accept or reject the proposal. If the Odelsting accepts the bill it is sent to the Lagting. If the latter body also accepts the bill it is then sent to the king (i.e., the government) for formal adoption. But the Lagting has two more options: it may reject the proposal totally, or it may suggest amendments to it. In both cases it is returned to the Odelsting for new consideration. The Odelsting may decide to stop the process, or accept the objections made by the Lagting. In the latter case the bill will go back to the Lagting, which may either reject or accept it in its revised form. In case of rejection, the bill will be presented to a plenary session of the Storting, but now a two-thirds majority is required for acceptance.

4. This distinction between material law and financial matters dates back to the 1830s when the Storting began the practice of dealing with financial and budgetary matters in plenary meeting. This was done in order to avoid the royal veto, which was restricted to material law.

5. In 1995 it was decided to experiment with open committee hearings. In 1999 a final decision will be made about the future of this innovation. So far the experiment seems to have been successful.

6. In his 1984 book *Der er det godt å sitte* (There it is good to sit), Guttorm Hansen, former president of the Storting and former parliamentary leader of the Labor Party, vividly described the activities and practices of the parliamentary parties (68–99).

7. Teigum (1995) analyzed the behavior of the two parties of the center, the Christian People's Party and the Center Party, between 1989 and 1993 and concluded that the two were nearly unanimous in their voting behavior for the entire period. In addition, she examined the written records of the two parties' group meetings. Also, a high degree of party cohesiveness could be detected, even though conflicts did arise on issues concerning public spending and private control. This degree of unity does not exist within the rank-and-file members of any of the parties (see chap. 7, below).

8. From 1981 until 1985 Norway was run by a bourgeois coalition. At the 1985 election the coalition lost its majority, but it continued as a minority coalition. In 1986, when this government was defeated, Labor took over as a minority government. It remained in power until 1989. After the election of 1989 a new bourgeois minority coalition took over. It remained in power for exactly one year. The Labor Party then formed a new minority government, which as of 1997 was still in power.

Chapter 5

Portions of this chapter are drawn from Valen (1988).

1. Norway, *Stortingsforhandlinger 1920* 3a. Ot. Prop. Nr. 1–50.

2. Paragraph 3 of the Act of Nomination specified that the number of delegates at provincial conventions range from 20 to 150, depending upon the number of votes the party received at the preceding Storting election. These seats are allocated to localities on the basis of the number of votes received in each locality at the last national election.

3. It was decided that neither sex should have less than 40 percent of the candidates on the list. The Socialist Left Party and the Liberal Party later decided that 50 percent of their candidates should be women.

4. It is not necessary to be a member of the Storting to be appointed to a cabinet position. Normally, about half of the cabinet ministers are members of the Storting. Those who are not often are elected to the Storting in subsequent years.

Chapter 6

1. Before 1938 national elections were held every three years.

2. Of course, these data alone do not prove this—the age differences in Table 6.3 could be explained by generational effects. Today's older people may have participated more when they were young. Our understanding of Norwegian politics suggests that increased participation with aging is a more plausible explanation.

Chapter 7

1. The very high intercorrelation of these variables rules out the use of multiple regression in sorting out the relative importance of parties, leaders, and issues as influences on the vote.

2. MacDonald et al. argue that this is a more satisfactory way to measure representativeness than spatial approaches.

Chapter 8

1. "The 'Feminization' of the Storting" was the title of a research project funded by the Norwegian Council for Applied Social Research. See Skjeie, 1988.

2. There is a very large literature on this subject, which we cannot summarize here. See Skard (1981), Nordisk Ministerrad (1983), Skjeie (1988, 1991, 1993), Nicholson (1993), Matland (1993, 1994, 1995), and sources cited therein.

3. Interviews were conducted in Oslo by Matthews in February 1991 with several of the prominent participants in this event, including Mrs. Brundtland.

4. The nonsocialist bloc, of course, contains parties that are highly rural (the Center Party and Christian People's Party) and urban (the Right and Progress parties). If this analysis were carried out within these parties rather than within the nonsocialist bloc the urban-rural differences might disappear. Unfortunately the party delegations in the Storting are too small to permit such an analysis.

Chapter 9

1. Hernes (1971) asked the same question in 1966. The results were: party, 66.7 percent; district, 30.6 percent; other responses/don't know, 27 percent. This suggests as much as a 10 percent decline in party orientation in twenty years.

2. Members of the two parties at the extremes of the ideological structure answered "yes" less often than the others, but the number of cases is too small to know if this is a genuine difference.

3. In 1985 the committee chairmanships were divided between the parties as follows:

Party	% Seats	% Chairmanships
SV	4	0
DNA	45	50
KrP	10	8
Sp	8	8
H	32	33
FrP	1	0

4. This finding is similar to that of Hernes (1971).

References

Aardal, Bernt. 1990. "Green Politics: A Norwegian Experience." *Scandinavian Political Studies* 13:147–64.

Aardal, Bernt, and Henry Valen. 1989. *Velgere, partier og politisk avstand* (Voters, parties and political distance). Oslo: Central Bureau of Statistics.

Achen, Christopher. 1977. "Measuring Representation: The Perils of the Correlation Coefficient." *American Journal of Political Science* 21:805–15.

———. 1978. "Measuring Representation." *American Journal of Political Science* 22:475–510.

Allen, Hillary. 1979. *Norway and Europe in the 1970's*. Oslo: Universitetsforlaget.

Almond, G. A., and J. Coleman. 1960. *The Politics of Developing Areas*. Princeton, N.J.: Princeton University Press.

American Political Science Association (APSA). Committee on Political Parties. 1950. *Toward a More Responsible Two-Party System. American Political Science Review* 44 (supplement).

Arnold, R. Douglas. 1993. "Can Inattentive Citizens Control Their Elected Representatives?" Pp. 401–16. in Lawrence C. Dodd and Bruce Oppenheimer, eds., *Congress Reconsidered*. 5th ed. Washington, D.C.: C.Q. Press.

Arter, David. 1984. *The Nordic Parliaments. A Comparative Analysis*. London: Hurst.

Arterton, Christopher. 1987. *Teledemocracy: Can Technology Protect Democracy?* Newbery Park, Calif.: Sage.

Barro, Robert J. 1973. "The Control of Politicians: An Economic Model." *Public Choice* 14:19–42.

Bennett, W. Lance. 1992. *The Governing Crisis: Media, Money and Marketing in American Elections*. New York: St. Martin's Press.

Bentley, Arthur F. 1935. *The Process of Government*. Bloomington, Ind.: Principia.

Berggrav, Dag. 1994. *Slik styres Norge* (Norway is governed like this). Oslo: Schibsted.

Bergmann, Torbjörn. 1993. "Formation Rules and Minority Governments." *European Journal of Political Research* 23:55–66.

Bjurulf, Bo, and Ingemar Glans. 1976. "Från Tvåblocksystem till Fraktionalisering. Partigruppers och Ledamöters Röstning I Norska Stortinget 1969–1974" (From two-bloc system to fractionalization. The voting record of party groups and individual MPs in the Norwegian Storting, 1969–1974). *Statsvitenskaplig tidsskrift* 79:231–53.

Budge, Ian, David Robertson, and Derek Hearl. 1987. *Ideology, Strategy and Party Change: Spatial Analyses of Post-War Election Programmes in 19 Democracies.* Cambridge: Cambridge University Press.

Burnham, Walter Dean. 1982. *The Current Crisis in American Politics.* New York: Oxford University Press.

Butler, David, and Austin Ranney, eds. 1994. *Referendums Around the World: The Growing Use of Direct Democracy.* Washington, D.C.: AEI Press.

Cain, Bruce, John Ferejohn, and Morris Fiorina. 1987. *The Personal Vote: Constituency Service and Electoral Independence,* Cambridge, Mass.: Harvard University Press.

Campbell, Angus, and Phillip Converse, Warren Miller, and Donald Stokes. 1960. *The American Voter.* New York: Wiley.

Carmines, Edward G., and James A. Stimson. 1989. *Issue Evolution: Race and the Transformation of American Politics.* Princeton, N.J.: Princeton University Press.

Central Bureau of Statistics, Oslo. 1986. *Stortingsvalget 1985* (The Storting election of 1985). Vol. 2.

Christophersen, Jens A. 1969. *Representant og velger* (Representative and voter). Oslo: Universitetsforlaget.

———. 1976. "Tilbake til det normale" (Back to normalcy). *Samtiden* 85(1):1–12.

Cnudde, Charles, and Donald McCrone. 1966. "The Linkage Between Constituency Attitudes and Congressional Voting Behavior." *American Political Science Review* 60:66–72.

Cronin, Thomas. 1989. *Direct Democracy: The Politics of Initiative, Referendum and Recall.* Cambridge, Mass.: Harvard University Press.

Dalton, Russell J. 1985. "Political Parties and Political Representation: Party Supports and Party Elites in Nine Nations." *Comparative Political Studies* 18: 267–99.

Dexter, Lewis Anthony. 1947. "The Representative and His District." *Human Organization* 16:2–13.

Downs, Anthony. 1957. *An Economic Theory of Democracy,* New York: Harper.

Duverger, Maurice. 1954 (first pub. 1951). *Political Parties: Their Organization and Activity in the Modern State.* London: Metheun.

Easton, David. 1966. *A Systems Analysis of Political Life.* New York: Wiley.

Eckstein, Harry. 1966. *Division and Cohesion in Democracy: A Study of Norway.* Princeton, N.J.: Princeton University Press.

Ehrenhalt, Alan. 1991. *The United States of Ambition: Politicians, Power, and the Pursuit of Office.* New York: Times Books.

Elder, N., A. H. Thomas, and D. Arter. 1982. *The Consensual Democracies? The Government and Politics of the Scandinavian States.* Oxford: Martin Robertson.

Epstein, Leon. 1967. *Political Parties in Western Democracies.* New York: Praeger.

Esaiasson, Peter, and Sören Holmberg. 1996. *Representation from Above: Members of Parliament and Representative Democracy in Sweden.* Aldershot: Dartmouth.

Eulau, Heinz, and Paul D. Karps. 1977. "The Puzzle of Representation: Specifying Components of Responsiveness." *Legislative Studies Quarterly* 2:233–54.

Eulau, Heinz, and Kenneth Prewitt. 1973. *Labyrinths of Democracy; Adaptions, Linkages, Representation, and Policies in Urban Politics.* Indianapolis: Bobbs, Merrill.

Eulau, Heinz, and John Wahlke, eds. 1978. *The Politics of Representation.* Beverly Hills, Calif.: Sage.

Fenno, Richard F., Jr. 1973. *Congressmen in Committees.* Boston: Little, Brown.

———. 1978. *Home Style: House Members in Their Districts.* Boston: Little, Brown.

Ferejohn, John. 1986. "Incumbent Performance and Electoral Control." *Public Choice* 50:5–25.

Fiorina, Morris. 1977. *Congress: Keystone of the Washington Establishment.* New Haven: Yale University Press.

———. 1981. *Retrospective Voting in American National Elections.* New Haven: Yale University Press.

Friedrick, Carl J. 1941. *Constitutional Government and Democracy.* Boston: Little, Brown.

Gallagher, M., and M. Marsh, eds. 1988. *Candidate Selection in Comparative Perspective.* London: Sage.

Grofman, Bernard, and Arend Lijphart, eds. 1986. *Electoral Laws and Their Political Consequences.* New York: Agathan Press.

Haavio-Mannilla, Elina. 1981. "The Position of Women." Chap. 24 in E. Allardt et al., eds., *Nordic Democracy.* Copenhagen: Det Danske Selskap.

Hall, Richard. 1996. *Participation in Congress.* New Haven: Yale University Press.

Hansen, Guttorm. 1984. *Der er det godt å sitte* (There it is good to sit). Oslo: Aschehoug.

Heidar, Knut. 1983. *Norske politiske facta 1884–1982* (Norwegian political facts 1884–1982). Oslo: Universitetsforlaget.

———. 1995a. "Partigruppene på Stortinget" (Party groups in the Storting). *Norsk Statsvitenskapelig tidsskrift* (Journal of Norwegian Political Science) 11:277–97.

———. 1995b. Norwegian Parliamentarians: What Do We Know and How Do We Know It? Revised version of paper presented at the Conference on the Political Roles of MPs in West European Countries, Vienna, Apr. 20–22, 1995.

———. 1996. Roles, Structures and Behavior: Norwegian Parliamentarians in the Nineties. Paper presented to the workshop on "Nordisk Parlamentsforskning," (Scandinavian Parliamentary research), Nordic Political Science Association Congress, Helsinki, Aug. 15–17, 1996.

Hellevik, Ottar. 1969. *Stortinget: En sosial elite?* (The Storting: a social elite?) Oslo: Pax.

Hernes, Gudmund 1971. *Interest, Influence and Cooperation: A Study of the Norwegian Parliament.* Ph.D. diss., Johns Hopkins University.

———. 1983. *Makt og styring* (Power and governing). Oslo: Gyldendal.

Hernes, Gudmund, and Kristine Nergaard. 1989. *Oss i mellom* (Between us). Oslo: FAFO.

Hjellum, T. 1967. "Politicalization of Local Governments." *Scandinavian Political Studies* 2:69–93.

Holmberg, Sören. 1974. *Riksdagen representerer svenska folket* (The Riksdag represents the Swedish people). Lund: Studentlitteratur.

———. 1989. "Political Representation in Sweden." *Scandinavian Political Studies* 12:1–36.

Holmberg, Sören, and Michael Giljam. 1987. *Väljare och val i Sverige* (Voters and elections in Sweden). Stockholm: Bonniers.

Iversen, Torben. 1994. "Political Leadership and Representation in West European Democracies: A Test of Three Models of Voting." *American Journal of Political Science* 38:45–74.

Jewell, Malcolm E. 1970. "Attitudinal Determinants of Legislative Behavior: The Utility of Role Analysis." Pp. 460–500 in A. Kornberg and L. D. Musolf, eds., *Legislatures in Developmental Perspective.* Durham, N.C.: Duke University Press.

———. 1985. "Legislators and Constituents in the Representative Process." Chap. 3 in Gerhard Loewenberg, Samuel C. Patterson, and Malcolm Jewell, eds., *Handbook of Legislative Research.* Cambridge, Mass.: Harvard University Press.

Karvonen, Lauri. 1993. "In from the Cold? Christian Parties in Scandinavia." *Scandinavian Political Studies* 16:25–48.

Key, V. O., Jr. 1949. *Southern Politics in State and Nation.* New York: Knopf.

———. 1958. *Parties, Politics and Pressure Groups.* 4th ed. New York: Crowell.

———. 1961. *Public Opinion and American Democracy.* New York: Knopf.

———. 1966. *The Responsible Electorate: Rationality in Presidential Voting, 1936–1960.* Cambridge, Mass.: Harvard University Press.

Kiewiet, D. Roderick, and McCubbins, Mathew D. 1991. *The Logic of Delegation: Congressional Parties and the Appropriations Process.* Chicago: University of Chicago Press.

King, Anthony. 1976. "Modes of Executive-Legislative Relations: Great Britain, France, and West Germany." *Legislative Studies Quarterly* 1:11–16.

Kingdon, John. 1966. *Candidates for Office.* New York: Random House.

Krehbiel, Keith. 1992. *Information and Legislative Organization.* Ann Arbor: University of Michigan Press.

Kristvik, Bjørn. 1953. *Partiene og valgordningen, 1885–1906* (The parties and the electoral system, 1885–1906). Master's diss., University of Oslo.

Kristvik, Bjørn, and Stein Rokkan. 1964. *Valgordningen* (The electoral system). Bergen: Chr. Michelsen Institute. Mimeo.

Kvavik, Robert. 1976. *Interest Groups in Norwegian Politics.* Oslo: Universitetsforlaget.

Lane, Jan-Erik, and Hanne Marthe Narud. 1994. "Maktfordelingsprinsippet og den Konstitusjonelle Teori: Spørsmålet om Bemanning av Statsmaktene." (The separation of powers and constitutional theory: The question of executive and legislative membership). In K. Midgaard and B. E. Rasch, eds., *Representativt Demokrati: Spilleregler under Debatt* (Representative Democracy: Rules under debate). Oslo: Universitetsforlaget.

Lijphart, Arend. 1984. *Democracies: Patterns of Majoritorian and Consensus Government in Twenty-One Countries.* New Haven: Yale University Press.

Listhaug, Ola. 1989. *Citizens, Parties and Norwegian Electoral Politics 1957–1985, An Empirical Study.* Trondheim: Tapir.

Listhaug, Ola, and Matti Wiberg. 1992. "Confidence in Political and Private Institutions." Paper presented at a meeting of the ESF-project, Beliefs in Government. Oxford University, Nov. 13–15, 1992.

Loewenberg, Gerhard, and Chong Lim Kim. 1978. "Comparing the Representativeness of Parliaments." *Legislative Studies Quarterly* 3:27–49.

MacDonald, Stuart E., Ola Listhaug, and George Rabinowitz. 1991. "Issues and Party Support in Multiparty Systems." *American Political Science Review* 85:1107–31.

Matland, Richard E. 1993. "Institutional Variables Affecting Female Representation in National Legislatures: The Case of Norway." *Journal of Politics* 55:737–55.

———. 1994. "Putting Scandinavian Equality to the Test: An Experimental Evaluation of Gender Stereotyping of Political Candidates in a Sample of Norwegian Voters." *British Journal of Political Science* 24:273–92.

———. 1995. "How the Election System Structure Has Helped Women Close the Representation Gap." In L. Karvonen and Per Selle, eds., *Women in Nordic Politics: Closing the Gap.* Brookfield, Vt.: Dartmouth Press.

Matthews, D. R. 1954. *The Social Background of Political Decision Makers.* Garden City, N.Y.: Doubleday.

———. 1960. *U.S. Senators and Their World.* Chapel Hill: University of North Carolina Press.

Matthews, Donald R., and James W. Prothro. 1966. *Negroes and the New Southern Politics.* New York: Harcourt, Brace, and World.

Matthews, Donald R., and James A. Stimson. 1975. *Yeas and Nays: Normal Decision-Making in the U.S. House of Representatives.* New York: Wiley-Interscience.

Mayhew, David. 1974. *Congress: The Electoral Connection.* New Haven: Yale University Press.

McKenzie, R. T. 1955. *British Political Parties.* New York: St. Martin's Press.

Michels, Robert. 1949, first pub. 1915. *Political Parties: A Sociological Study of the Oligarchical Tendencies of Modern Democracy.* Glencoe. Ill.: Free Press.

Miller, Arthur. 1974. "Political Issues and Trust in Government 1964–1974." *American Political Science Review* 68:951–72.

Miller, Arthur, and Ola Listhaug. 1990. "Political Parties and Confidence in Government: A Comparison of Norway, Sweden and the United States." *British Journal of Political Science* 29:357–86.

Miller, Warren E., and Donald Stokes. 1963. "Constituency Influence in Congress." *American Political Science Review* 57:45–56.

Narud, Hanne Marthe. 1994. "Nominasjoner og pressen" (Nominations and the press). In Knut Heidar and Lars Svaasand, eds., *Partiene I en brytningstid* (Parties in a time of conflict). Bergen: Alma Mater.

————. 1996a. "Party Policies and Government Accountability." *Party Policies* 2(4):479–506.

————. 1996b. *Voters, Parties and Governments.* Report 96:7. Oslo: Institute for Social Research.

Narud, Hanne Marthe, and Henry Valen. 1996. "Decline of Electoral Turnout: The Case of Norway." *European Journal of Political Research* 29:235–56.

Nicholson, Beryl. 1993. "From Interest Group to (Almost) Equal Citizenship: Women's Representation in the Norwegian Parliament." *Parliamentary Affairs* 46:255–63.

Nordby, Trond. 1994. *Korporatisme på norsk, 1920–1990* (Corporatism in Norway, 1920–1990). Oslo: Universitetsforlaget.

Nordisk Ministerrad. 1983. *Det uferdige demokratiet: Kvinner i nordisk politikk* (The unfinished democracy: Women in Nordic politics). Oslo: Nordisk Ministerrad.

Norway. 1920. *Stortingsforhandlinger* (Record of *Storting* negotiations).

Norway. 1920. *Valgordningskommisjon av 1917* (Electoral Commission of 1917). Report 1. Published as appendix to Ot. Prop. Nr. 37. Oslo: The Storting.

Norway, Central Bureau of Statistics. 1959–95. *Election Statistics for Commune Elections.*

Norway. 1903. *Instilling fia Valgordningskommisjon av 1900* (Report from the Electoral Commission of 1900). Published in Storting Prop. Nr. 76 of 1903–4. Oslo: The Storting.

Olsen, Johan P. 1983. *Organized Democracy: Political Institutions in a Welfare State— The Case of Norway.* Oslo: Universitetsforlaget.

Olson, Mancur, Jr. 1965. *The Logic of Collective Action.* Cambridge, Mass.: Harvard University Press.

Parker, Glenn. 1992. *Institutional Change, Discretion, and the Making of Modern Congress: An Economic Interpretation.* Ann Arbor: University of Michigan Press.

Patterson, Samuel C., Randall B. Ripley, and Stephen V. Quinlan. 1991. "Citizens' Orientations Toward Legislatures: Congress and the State Legislature." *Western Political Quarterly* 44:315–38.

Pennock, Roland, and John Chapman, eds. 1968. *Representation*. New York: Atherton.

Pitkin, Hanna F. 1967. *The Concept of Representation*. Berkeley: University of California Press.

Powell, Bingham. 1986. "American Voter Turnout in Comparative Perspective." *American Political Science Review* 80:17–43.

Putnam, Robert D. 1976. *The Comparative Study of Political Elites*. Englewood Cliffs, N.J.: Prentice-Hall.

Rabinowitz, George. 1978. "On the Nature of Political Issues: Insights from a Spatial Analysis." *American Journal of Political Science* 22:793–817.

Rabinowitz, George and Stuart E. MacDonald. 1989. "A Directional Theory of Issue Voting." *American Political Science Review* 83:93–121.

Rabinowitz, George, Stuart E. MacDonald, and Ola Listhaug. 1991. "New Players in an Old Game: Party Strategy in Multi-Party Systems." *Comparative Political Studies* 24:147–85.

Ranney, Austin. 1962. *The Doctrine of Responsible Party Government: Its Origins and Present State*. Urbana: University of Illinois Press.

Ranney, Austin, and Willmore Kendall. 1956. *Democracy and the American Party Systems*. New York: Harcourt, Brace.

Rasch, Bjørn Erik. 1994. "Question Time in the Norwegian Storting: Theoretical and Empirical Considerations." In M. Wiberg, ed., *Parliamentary Control in the Nordic Countries*. Helsinki: Finnish Political Science Association.

Rokkan, Stein. 1966. "Norway: Numerical Democracy and Corporate Pluralism." Chap. 3 in Robert Dahl, ed., *Political Oppositions in Western Democracies*. New Haven: Yale University Press.

———. 1967. "Geography, Religion and Social Class: Cross-Cutting Cleavages in Norwegian Politics." Pp. 367–444 in S. M. Lipset and S. Rokkan, eds., *Party Systems and Voters Alignments: Cross-National Perspectives*. New York: Free Press.

———. 1970. *Citizens, Elections, Parties*. Bergen: Universitetsforlaget.

Rokkan, Stein, and Henry Valen. 1962. "The Mobilization of the Periphery." In S. Rokkan, ed., *Approaches to the Study of Political Participation*. Bergen: Chr. Mickelson Institutt.

———. 1964. "Regional Contrasts in Norwegian Politics." In Eric Allardt and Yrjö Littunen, eds., *Changes, Ideologies and Party Systems*. Helsinki: Westermark Society.

Rommetvedt, Hilmar. 1991. "Partiavstand og Partikoalisjoner" (Party distances and party coalitions). Ph.D. diss., University of Bergen.

———. 1992. "Norway: From Consensual Majority Parliamentarism to Dissensual Minority Parliamentarism." Pp. 51–97 in Erik Damgaard, ed., *Parliamentary Change in the Nordic Countries*. Oslo: Universitetsforlaget.

Ross, Alf. 1946. *Hvorfor demokrati?* (Why democracy?). Copenhagen: Munksgaard.

Rule, Wilma. 1987. "Electoral Systems, Contextual Factors and Women's Opportunity for Election to Parliament in 23 Democracies." *Western Political Quarterly* 40:477–98.

Rusk, John, and Ola Borre. 1976. "The Changing Party Space in Danish Voting Perceptions 1971–73." In J. Budge, J. Crewe, and D. Farlie, eds., *Party Identification and Beyond*. London: Wiley.

Schmitter, Philippe. 1974. "Still the Century of Corporatism?" *Review of Politics* 36:75–131.

Seip, Jens Arup. 1963. *Fra embedsmannsstat til ettpartistat og andre essays* (From civil service state to one party state and other essays). Oslo: Universitetsforlaget.

Sejersted, F. 1984. *Høyres historie* (The history of Høyre). Vol. 3. Oslo: Cappelen.

Shaffer, William. 1991. "Interparty Spatial Relationships in Norwegian Roll Call Votes." *Scandinavian Political Studies* 14:59–83.

Skard, Torild. 1981. "Progress for Women: Increased Female Representation in Political Elites in Norway." Chap. 5 in C. F. Epstein and R. L. Coser, eds., *Access to Power: Cross National Studies of Women and Elites*. London: Allen and Unwin.

Skard, Torild, and Elina Haavio-Mannila. 1984. "Equality Between the Sexes— Myth or Reality in Norden?" *Daedalus* 113:141–67.

Skjeie, Hege. 1988. *The Feminization of Power: Norway's Political Experiment (1986–)*. Report 88: 8. Oslo: Institute for Social Research.

———. 1991. "The Rhetoric of Difference: On Women's Inclusion into Political Elites." *Politics and Society* 19:133–63.

———. 1993. "Ending the Male Hegemony: The Norwegian Experience." Chap. 10 in J. Lovenduski and P. Norris, eds., *Gender and Party Politics*. London: Sage.

Stimson, James A. 1991. *Public Opinion in America: Moods, Cycles and Swings*. Boulder, Colo.: Westview Press.

Strøm, Kaare. 1984. "Minority Governments in Parliamentary Democracies." *Comparative Political Studies* 17:199–227.

———. 1990. *Minority Government and Majority Rule*. Cambridge: Cambridge University Press.

Strøm, Kaare, and Jørn Y. Leipart. 1989. "Ideology, Strategy and Party Competition in Postwar Norway." *European Journal of Political Research* 17:263–88.

Svåsand, Lars. 1994. "Change and Adaptation in Party Organizations: The Case of Norway." In Richard S. Katz and Peter Mair, eds., *How Parties Organize*. London: Sage.

Taagepera, Rein, and Matthew Shugart. 1989. *Seats and Votes: The Effects and Determinants of Electoral Systems*. New Haven: Yale University Press.

Teigum, Hanne Marit. 1995. *Representasjon i en flerdimensjonal konfliktstruktur* (Representation in a multi-dimensional conflict structure). Master's thesis, University of Bergen.

Thomassen, Jacques. 1994. "Empirical Research into Political Representation: Failing Democracy or Failing Models." In M. Kent Jennings and Thomas E. Mann, eds., *Elections at Home and Abroad*. Ann Arbor: University of Michigan Press.

Torp, Olaf, ed. 1990. *Stortinget i navn og tall 1989–93* (The Storting in names and numbers, 1989–93). Oslo: Universitetsforlaget.

Truman, David B. 1951. *The Governmental Process*. New York: Knopf.

Uslaner, Eric. 1993. *The Decline of Comity in Congress*. Ann Arbor: University of Michigan Press.

Valen, H. 1986. "The Storting Election of September 1985: The Welfare State Under Pressure." *Scandinavian Political Studies* 9(2):177–88.

———. 1988. "Norway: Decentralization and Group Representation." In M. Gallagher and M. Marsh, eds., *Candidate Selection in Comparative Perspective*. London: Sage.

———. 1989. "Kvinder selv stod upp og strede" (Also the women stood up and fought). Pp. 96–107 in R. Hirsti, ed., *Gro midt i livet* (Gro in the middle of life: A festschrift for Gro Harlem Brundtland). Oslo: Tiden.

———. 1990. "Coalitions and Political Distances." In B. Sänkiatio et al., eds., *People and Their Politics*. Helsinki: Finnish Political Science Association.

———. 1994. "List Alliances: An Experiment in Political Representation." Pp. 289–332 in M. Kent Jennings and Thomas E. Mann, eds., *Elections at Home and Abroad*. Ann Arbor: University of Michigan Press.

Valen, H., and B. Aardal. 1983. *Et valg i perspetiv: En studie av stortingsvalget in 1981* (An election in perspective: A study of the 1981 Storting election). Oslo: Bureau of Statistics.

Valen, Henry, Bernt Aardal, and Gunnar Vogt. 1990. *Endring og Kontinuitet: Stortingsvalget 1989* (Continuity and change: The Storting election of 1989). Oslo: Bureau of Statistics.

Valen, Henry, and Daniel Katz. 1964. *Political Parties in Norway*. Oslo: Universitetsforlaget.

Valen, Henry, and Stein Rokkan. 1974. "Norway: Conflict Structure and Mass Politics in a European Periphery." In R. Rose, ed., *Comparative Electoral Behavior*. New York: Free Press.

Verba, Sidney, and Norman H. Nie. 1972. *Participation in America: Political Democracy and Social Equality*. New York: Harper and Row.

Wahlke, John C. 1971. "Policy Demands and System Support: The Role of the Represented." *British Journal of Political Science* 1:271–90.

———. 1978. "Policy Demands and System Support: The Role of the Represented." In H. Eulau and J. C. Wahlke, eds., *The Politics of Representation*. Beverly Hills, Calif.: Sage.

Wahlke, John, and Heinz Eulau, William Buchanan, and LeRoy C. Ferguson. 1962. *The Legislative System*. New York: Wiley.

Wattenberg, Martin. 1986. *The Decline of American Political Parties, 1952–1984.* Cambridge, Mass.: Harvard University Press.

Weissberg, Robert. 1978. "Collective vs. Dyadic Representation in Congress." *American Political Science Review* 72:535–47.

———. 1979. "Assessing Legislator-Constituency Policy Agreement." *Legislative Studies Quarterly* 4:605–22.

Index

Parliaments and Legislatures Series

OTHER BOOKS IN THE SERIES